A Bear of My Own

Manual For Bearmaking and Designing

by Rotraud Ilisch

Dedication

I would like to thank my daughters, Maja and Anna, who competently critiqued my text, and most of all my husband, who can't make bears, but taught me to handle the computer. Without his help, this book could not have been written.

Merfeld, Germany, April 1996
© 1996 Rotraud Ilisch

Acknowledgments

As soon as I introduced this book at "Teddy Total" in Hennef, Germany in 1996, some American friends asked for an English translation. The book became a success in Germany and finally my daughter Maja translated it.

Special thanks to Friedel Rowe in England, Debbi Henretty in the USA and Jacqui Young in Canada who thoughtfully revised the translation.

Thanks to Anna's friend, Lars Wege, for photographing material and some of the bears.

If not mentioned otherwise, all bears, photographs, and drawings were made by the author.

Merfeld, Germany, July 1998
© 1998 Rotraud Ilisch for the English translation

Additional copies of this book may be purchased from
Hobby House Press, Inc.
1 Corporate Drive
Grantsville, Maryland 21536
1-800-554-1447
or from your favorite bookstore or dealer.

© 1998 Rotraud Ilisch for the English translation
Rotraud Ilisch   Antoniusstr. 11   D- 48249 Dülmen   Germany
Tel +49 2594 81745 Fax +49 2594 84488
e-mail baer.co@t-online.de
http://home.t-online.de/home/baer.co

Printed in the United States of America

ISBN: 0-87588-544-6

Table of Contents

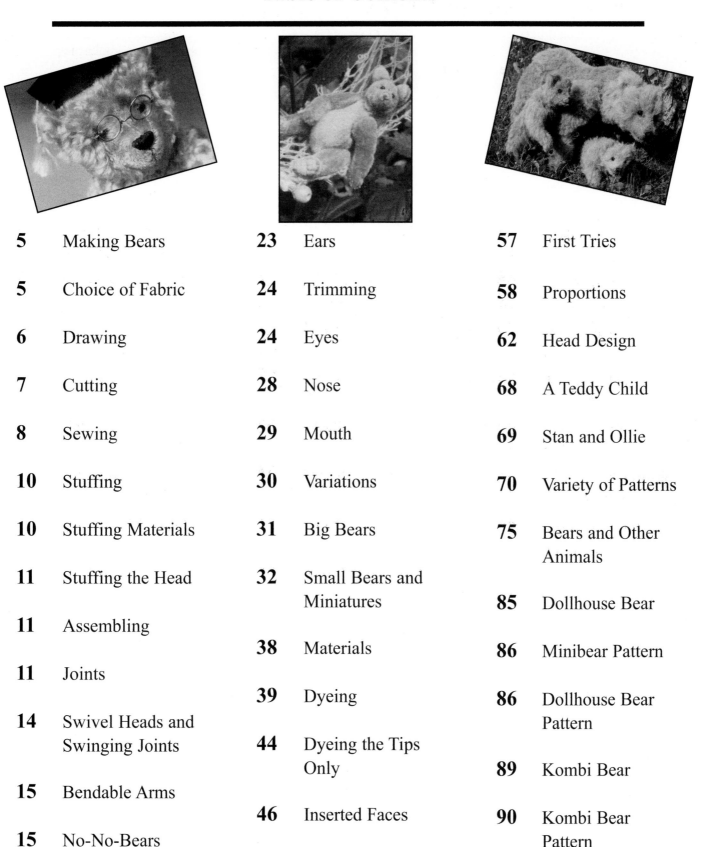

A Bear Of My Own

1. "Lieschen."

This is "Lieschen," or "Lizzy" in English. I made her in 1987 as a Christmas gift for my youngest son Josef and I was as proud of her as you must have been of your own first bear. "Lieschen" was accepted enthusiastically, resulting in far more than 800 bears of my making following her.

Regarding "Lieschen" critically, however, I must admit she's not perfect. Only over time have I learned how to make really good bears, and I'm still learning. Watching my bear-making daughters, I noticed that they were able to make very good bears in a far shorter amount of time. That's no wonder, since a perfectionist mother guided them.

I assume that you already know about the basics of bear making and have produced at least one, and more likely a couple of bears. Maybe you've been hit by real "bear-mania" and are now trying all the new patterns you can get your hands on, as I did in my beginning. Perhaps you wish to make your very own bears, with your own design.

I'd like to offer my help on your way to design a bear of your own. I've held a lot of classes, teaching bear making to people from 10 to 80 years old. Today, I'm still in touch with a number of former students as well as other beginners and advanced bear makers. I try to give them tips and advice for making better bears, and they also share their ideas with me.

In my experience, there are common mistakes for many new bear makers. For example, a lot of beginners are uncertain about where to put eyes, ears and nose. Before I turn to designing patterns, in the first part of this manual I'd like to point out mistakes in bear making and how to avoid them. Be assured that I made the greater part of these mistakes myself (as shown on some photographs). Of course, my concepts of improvement are all subjective, resulting from my personal view of a beautiful teddy bear. Maybe your ideas are similar.

Making Bears

I assume that you have at least one teddy pattern (more likely a few) and already know the basic routine of bear making. Nevertheless, I'd like to guide you through the process of making a teddy and touch upon the single steps.

Don't be surprised if I frequently point out how features look on real bears – and you don't want to make Ursus Arctos, but Teddy Bear! Maybe you already know that Richard Steiff, the inventor of teddy bears, first watched bears in the zoo and sketched them before designing the first teddy. It is always useful to keep the true model of teddies in mind -- the wild bears.

Choice of Fabric

Your choice of fabric depends on your personal taste and your financial resources. I believe that it pays to make a teddy, which is a lot of work, out of a high quality fabric like mohair. I used to work with synthetics in my beginner classes, but later on I let beginners work with mohair as well. The bears simply turned out more beautiful. Of course that's relative – a good bear made with synthetics is always more beautiful than one made badly of mohair.

If possible, don't use stretchy, Jersey-backed fabric. It's predestined for trouble, because stuffing too hard can make the whole bear lose its shape. Nearly all fabrics with a knitted backing are more or less elastic, but this may be overcome by ironing cambric coated with textile glue to the backing or you may wish to try a sewable interfacing.

Synthetic fabrics can be very different in both quality and price. There are some high quality fabrics with woven backings that are similar to real fur and may produce very nice bears. These fabrics usually have a dense fur, and are not very easy to work with. Most are very slippery, so you will have to baste or use a lot of pins.

Another disadvantage of synthetic plush is that it will lose its nice look with age, whereas mohair or even viscose plush will get back its old shine after cleaning. Viscose plush is a silky fabric that was used for cheap teddies. It very often comes in bright colors and also may be dyed. It is a bit slippery and hard to work with, but is available in different piles and is not very expensive. I think you should use it only for very special projects.

Cotton plush was also used for cheap teddies in the fifties. It comes in yellow shades most of the time, may also be dyed and gives bears a vintage touch. I don't recommend the cotton plush with knitted backing, but the cotton plush with woven backing is nice to work with.

I prefer fabrics made with animal hair. You can use real fur from old coats, but it is always hard to work with real fur. However, mink is better than rabbit, which has a very thin skin. You always need an interfacing because you can easily destroy the skin while stuffing. Real fur, especially sheepskin, can break with age. Without interfacing it is impossible to repair.

The hair of animals, woven into a backing of wool or cotton, is good for bear making. Sheep wool is fairly inexpensive and nice to work with. It comes as plush with cotton backing and as wool fabric with very short pile for coats. There is also camel hair (from llamas). Maybe you will find an old coat of camel hair - enough fabric for several bears of high quality. Fraying may be a problem, so you should use fray stop at the edges.

Alpaca is usually a very dense plush with cotton backing. The wool of alpacas, a small kind of llama, is very smooth and a little bit silky. Alpaca plush comes with long and short pile and is nice for bears. I like it very much for my realistic bears, but sometimes it is hard to get.

Mohair plush is made from the hair of angora goats with cotton backing added. It is the classic material for teddies and will keep its shine for decades, although some teddies have lost most of their hair. Mohair is usually the most expensive fabric, depending on the length and the density of its pile. The hair length may vary from 1/8-inch to 3-inch and may be very dense and fluffy or comes as "sparse mohair" with very little mohair woven in.

Drawing

Work with the pattern you are familiar with or use the one you will find in this book. If you are instructed to sew in the ears before stuffing, I advise against it, because it robs you of your own choice of where to put them. If there is an opening for the ears, simply leave it out. If the ears are to be sewn into darts, draw the darts and close them during sewing without inserting the ears.

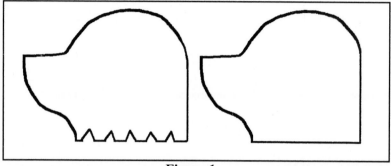

Figure 1.

Some patterns have the lower edge of the head as a zigzag line. In my experience, this doesn't give any improvements. I think that a head with straight edges is easier to sew up (see Fig. 1).

There are also patterns that leave the upper part of the body open to glue in the neck disk. I think it is easier to sew up the whole upper section of the body and never to work with glue inside a bear.

Make stencils of thin cardboard (e.g. from empty cereal boxes) to draw the pieces of your pattern onto the fabric. Quilters' plastic also works very well. Since it is transparent, you can lay it on the original pattern, draw the lines and cut out the pieces.

To draw on the fabric, use a soft pencil, biro or waterproof marker. Make sure it will not bleed out when it comes in contact with water. With a dark fabric, a white or yellow crayon, slightly moistened, works well. There are also special pens for drawing on dark fabric. You will get the clearest and most visible lines on dark fabric by using metallic gold or silver markers.

Before you start transferring your pattern onto the fabric using the stencils, note the nap direction on the backside of your fabric. If the nap is not marked on the pieces of your pattern, imagine stroking the finished teddy. You'd stroke the back from neck to tail and the arms and legs from joint to paws.

On the head, the hairs run from the tip of the nose towards the neck, which is obvious with the head gusset. There are different ways to draw the sides of the head (see Fig.2), so you should try to do it in the way that uses the least material. Just be careful that both sides of the head have the same nap direction. Mind the ears – they have the hairs running towards the tips, so when drawing, the ears must have the curve pointing in the nap direction.

If you have a leftover piece of fabric large enough for your bear but the nap is going the wrong way, you may change this by wetting the fabric and hanging it out to dry with the hair pointing the right way. If need be, you can also moisten the fur of a finished bear with the help of a steam iron or steam cleaner and brush the hairs into the right direction. This works only with mohair, not synthetics.

A seam allowance of $^1/_4$ inch (0.65 cms) is usual, so a finger's width of space between the pattern pieces is fine. If the seam allowance is already included in the pattern, the pieces may touch. I have seen beginners working rather lavishly with their material when drawing and cutting. My daughter Maja once collected the leftovers of a very expensive distressed piece of mohair after a workshop and made a 10-inch bear out of them.

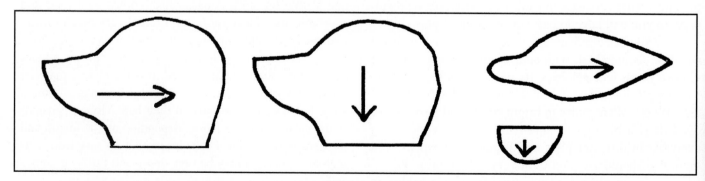

Figure 2.

Some fabrics have backing that tends to unravel after cutting. In these cases, a generous seam allowance is advisable. Liquids such as "fray check" can be used to avoid unraveling. American bear makers taught me a trick to reduce fraying. After drawing the edges, use a paintbrush to go over them with white glue dissolved in water. After drying, the edges will be a little bit stiffer than before and can be cut without fraying.

Use high-quality material, but be thrifty when cutting out your pattern. Perhaps the off-cuts will do for a smaller bear, or you can use them for the muzzle and inner ears of a bear of a different color. Throw away only the tiny pieces and collect all mohair leftovers. It could happen that a bear you give away gets in a brawl with a dog and is afterwards missing an ear or has a hole in its fur. Or perhaps your neighbors find out that you make bears and their bears become your first patients for surgery.

If your pattern comes with instructions showing how to lay out the pieces, you can use them, but usually there are lots of possibilities for economical drawing. For example, you may follow the curve of the tummy with an arm. Draw the ears last, since there are often suitable spaces left in between the other pieces. You don't have to mind the nap direction precisely– if it works out easier, it is all right if it follows the general direction.

Many teddy patterns have a body consisting of four parts. In my opinion, it takes less effort to sew a two-part body. If you put the parts of the pattern together as shown in the illustration, you get a two-part-pattern for the body. On the other hand, you may just get a very narrow piece of fabric. Then you may have to divide a two-part body into four.

The same is true for arms and legs if they consist of only one part (Fig. 3). I usually prefer two-part arms to work with. I think it is easier to sew the paw first on the inner arm and then sew both pieces together. When I design an arm, I draw the outer arm, mark the line for the paw and then bend the arm at this line. Then I can use only one piece for drawing all three parts of the arm. I usually also draw only one side of the leg. If it is straight, then I can mirror it while drawing on the fabric.

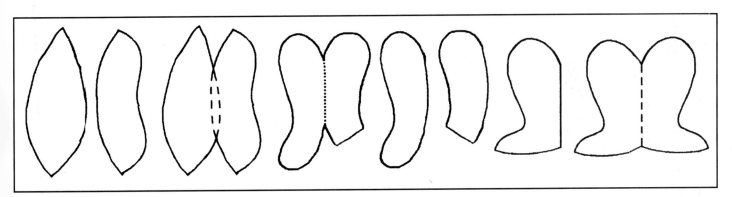

Figure 3.

Cutting

Before you start cutting, check carefully to be sure all the pieces are drawn the right way, in the correct number and are facing each other. It's always annoying to find out that you have cut two right arms, but no left one.

Always cut very carefully. Uneven pieces are nearly always a nuisance when sewing. Use small, sharp, pointy scissors and cut only the backing of the fabric, not the entire fur. This is done to avoid shorter hairs at the seams, and it looks nicer on the finished teddy.

You may give your bears felt paws like those of classical teddies. You will, however, have to put up with the paws wearing out as easily as those of classic teddies did (and as a teddy doctor I can tell you a thing or two about that). Velour and ultrasuede will last longer. I myself prefer real leather, which I collected in a variety of colors, since I bought a number of old leather jackets at flea markets. If you happen to have dogs and/or cats, test them to see how they behave towards leather – some pets mistake teddy's paws for their own chewing bones.

Sewing

Here you will find all the stitches required for bear making.

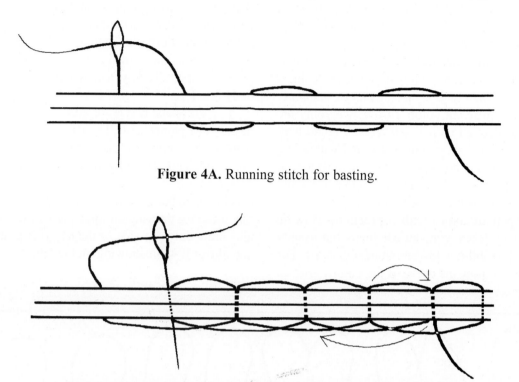

Figure 4A. Running stitch for basting.

Figure 4B. Double running stitch for inserting soles or special parts.

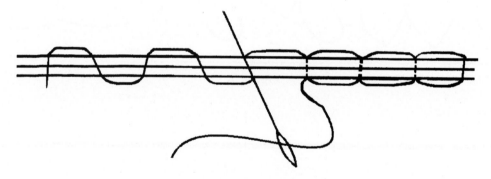

Figure 4C. Backstitch for sewing by hand.

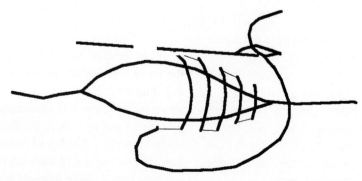

Figure 4D. Ladder stitch for closing all openings and sewing on the ears.

Apart from the really tiny ones, most teddy bears are stitched up by machine. I assume that you do the same, unless you do not have access to a sewing machine. If you have never worked with one before, it's easier to learn than to sew the whole bear by hand. By making bears, my children learned how to work with a sewing machine.

Sewing the bear by hand will not improve its quality, and it is very time consuming, since the stitches must be very short to withstand the stress of stuffing. Even a machine-sewn bear still requires a lot of hand stitching in the making. However, sewing by hand is a very leisurely kind of work which you can do while watching TV or looking after your children.

There's no rule about which part to start sewing first. Usually, the pieces must be pinned together before sewing, depending on how slippery the fabric is. When sewing the head, the neck seam is closed first. It's advisable to baste the gusset first (see basting stitch, Fig. 4a) so it won't slip away and so the head turns out symmetrically. The same rule applies to the soles of the feet: baste them in by hand, then sew by machine. I insert the soles with the leg standing upright and the sole pointing down. If you are making very small bears, insert the soles all by hand. In this case, I don't use the backstitch (Fig. 4b), but a double basting stitch, i.e. I baste all around the sole, then go for a second lap, closing the gaps of the first one (Fig. 4c).

If the ears are very small and could slip when sewing, you can fold the fabric right sides together, draw and sew the ears, and then cut them. I also use this method when sewing rather small bears by machine.

For all kinds of bears, it is advisable to sew up the bottom of the ears with a zigzag stitch after turning them inside out. This makes them easier to sew to the head. Never stuff the ears!

Before turning the finished parts right side out, look at the back side of the seams. Sometimes the fabric slips, leaving gaps. These mistakes are easily corrected by sewing a second time, back side up. The seam must be undone only if the discrepancy is very significant. By the way, an ordinary straight stitch will do. Unlike stuffed dolls, teddies must not be sewn with a zigzag stitch.

Don't forget to leave open gaps when sewing arms, legs and back. You'll need at least as much space as the size of the disk to insert it.

Maybe someone has told you a "great trick": first sew all around the arms and legs, then slit the fabric where the disk is going to be. Next, turn the piece and stuff through the slit (Fig. 5). Several teddy bear companies used this method for years because it is faster and the arms and legs bear no visible hand seams. However, this resulted in many teddies losing their limbs. Each movement of the joint strains the hand seams with which the slit is finally closed after inserting the disk and cotter pin. Frequently, the seam opens and the slit elongates, and suddenly a handshake with Teddy ends up with you shaking the entire arm, which has fallen off. To repair it, you'll have to open the body – otherwise, you couldn't reach the joints. I've had to do this operation so often that I can only tell you to stay away from tricks like this. In any case, you'll have to sew up the back by hand, so you must learn the essential ladder stitch (Fig. 4d).

The arms are always closed on the back side. With the legs, seam placement depends on the pattern. If the leg was placed on a fold and cut in one piece, the seam is on the front, of course. Otherwise, it is on the back.

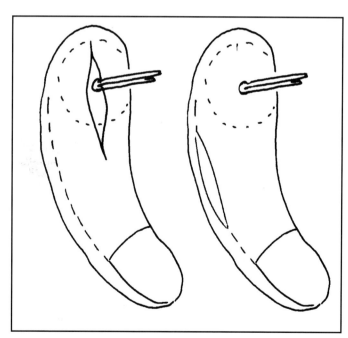

Figure 5. Don't do this.   Better this.

Stuffing

Before turning the parts of a bear inside out, Debbi Henretty taught me to pick the hairs out of the seam using a comb or a long needle. By doing this, you prevent short hairs from coming out of the seams after turning. They don't look nice and it is impossible to get rid of them after turning. This technique helps to make seams nearly invisible in mohair.

After turning the pieces inside out, the project grows more interesting, for now the head is to be stuffed.

Stuffing Materials

This leaves the question: what to stuff with? Here, the opinions differ. Many swear by wood-wool (excelsior), the classical working material, while others prefer fiberfill or wool. I myself use wood-wool for restoring old teddies, but usually not for stuffing new ones. In my opinion, wood-wool has no advantages apart from being rather light and classical. It's unsuitable for clean work, since your clothing and the floor will always get their share. Furthermore, it's not very durable. The teddy must be kept away from both moisture and dry heat, because the wooden shavings tend to turn brittle and break. In the worst cases, they turn into a kind of sawdust, and the bear's body simply collapses.

If you'd like to work with wood-wool, however, use the refined kind made especially for stuffing bears. Wood-wool as it's used for packing glasses is far too rough to use as teddy bear stuffing.

It is recommended that the wood-wool lay outdoors for a night to make it smoother to work with. Unfortunately, this is not always possible. My fellow bear maker Friedel Rowe suggests moistening the wood-wool with a spray bottle before use, but only slightly since the wood-wool must not get wet.

Here's another bit of advice from bear maker Claudia Weinstein: if your filling material is so dense that you can't get a needle through it when stitching the nose, stuff the tip of the nose with wood-wool thus and the needle will glide though easily.

The most common stuffing material is synthetic fiberfill. You need not buy the expensive layer wadding as used for making dolls, since ordinary flock wadding will work just as well. However, the brands differ in quality. With some, it's hard to get the awl through the head when inserting the eyes.

Unspun wool is also very good as a stuffing material, with the aforesaid problem never occurring. However, it is rather expensive when purchased in small bags in hobby stores. It is less expensive if you can get it straight from the keeper, which works well because bear stuffing doesn't require the quality of spinnable wool. Maybe you'll get your wool fresh from the sheep: greasy and full of dirt. You can put it into a net and wash it in your machine on the wool cycle two or three times so that the dirt is completely washed out. Then run it through the spin cycle and dry it in the dryer or the open air.

When working with wool, some bear makers wrap small amounts of dried lavender blossoms in cloth bags and put them into all parts of the teddy's body. Besides the bear spreading a pleasant odor for quite a time, this also keeps away moths.

Dog owners should test out their dog's reaction towards sheep wool before using it. One method is to stuff wool into a (clean) stocking and watch if the dog leaves it alone or tries to rip it into pieces.

Common surgical cotton is not suitable for stuffing, since it tends to get lumpy.

During recent years, plastic pellets have become more and more popular as a filling for teddy bears, and are usually combined with fiberfill. Pellets are produced in a variety of sizes and materials such as plastic or glass. If the feet are heavy enough, a pellet-stuffed bear may be able to stand without help. However, pellets cannot be used for stuffing the head. Pellets are produced in a variety of sizes and materials such as plastic or glass

Some bear makers also use steel shot for stuffing. **Never use lead shot. It is toxic and may cause severe health problems!**

A funnel is usually needed to pellet-fill the body. Pour carefully – there is no fun in picking up a load of pellets from the floor! I myself don't use pellets because I don't like the touch of them – it feels as if the bear has its belly full of buckshot. I don't see the advantage of a teddy being rather heavy, but many bear makers and collectors swear by it. I prefer the feeling of the very tiny glass beads some bear makers use now. If you want to use them, make sure your seams are well sewn and use tiny stitches to prevent the glass beads from leaking out.

Do not use materials such as cat litter to make your bear heavy. Also avoid seeds. They work nicely, but may contain bugs and would also cause problems if the bear should become wet.

Stuffing the Head

After this close-up on materials, let's return to your bear. You must be very careful when stuffing, especially with the head. The rule is not "fill in as long as there's room for more" since even a well-sewn head will lose its shape if overstuffed. Some teddies' heads then look as if they have been over-inflated.

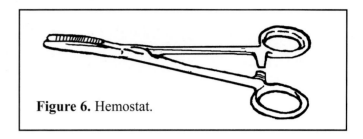

Figure 6. Hemostat.

Stuff the nose first and take care that the tip is filled tightly, since it's hard to reach this spot afterwards. When the whole head is somewhat well-filled, continue stuffing by placing the material in the right spots, thus molding the head. Find out where more filling is needed by exploring with your fingers, then add it in small amounts. In most cases, you'll need a helping tool. For larger bears, a special stuffing tool or the handle of a wooden spoon or screwdriver works well. For small bears, a hemostat (Fig. 6) will take the stuffing where it's needed. Hemostats come in various shapes and sizes. Be careful not to get one with sharp ends that could tear your fabric.

Test: is the muzzle well stuffed? Is there a lack of filling in the back of the head or the cheeks? Most important: is the head symmetrical? Depending on the stuffing, the same head can look quite different, so at this stage, you should already have an idea about the shape of the head.

Take care to leave enough space to insert the head disk in the neck opening and don't stuff so tightly that the head can't be sewn up afterwards.

If your bear is 15 inches (38 cms) or larger, you should continue finishing the head. Otherwise, you'll have the entire big bear on your lap when sewing on the ears or stitching the nose. Of course, you can also finish the head now if your bear is smaller, but I think of the finishing touches to the face as a sort of highlight and save them for last.

Assembling

Joints

At this stage, we need to take a closer look at disk joints. The market offers a large variety. Unfortunately, pre-combined sets of disks are often of little use. The sets offering five disks of equal size are unsuitable: for most bears, you'll need at least two different sizes, as the thighs of the bear are usually wider than the upper arms. Thus, disks that fit the arms are often too small for the legs, creating the effect of enormous hips. Even more miserable is the look of a bear with a neck disk that is too small, making the neck look lean as if the bear has been strangled. This problem can only be disguised with a scarf (Fig. 7).

There is no rule that an 11-inch (28 cm) bear requires 1.7-inch (4.5 cm) disks for the legs and neck and 1.3-inch (3.5 cm) disks for the arms. The size of the disks always depends on the pattern. The disk should fill the curve of the upper arm or leg and needs only a small amount of looseness. For bears from 7-1/2 inches (19 cms) to 11 inches (28 cms), 0.2 inches (.5 cms) will do quite well, while 0.4 inches (1 cm) is fine for larger bears. With most bears, the size of the leg disk equals the neck, but of course, there are exceptions.

Figure 7.

Top Left and Right:
2. Cardboard disks, washers and cotter pins come in various sizes. Photograph by Lars Wege.

3. Plastic joints with a metal washer. *Photograph by Lars Wege.*

I used to work with different kinds of plastic joints, with the advantage of the bear becoming machine-washable. But they also have disadvantages, apart from being rather expensive. First, they are available only in a few sizes. Second, they very often don't stay as tight as they should. Rubber washers especially tend to loosen. Metal washers, on the other hand, stay dead tight, which is quite a problem if you'd like to disassemble a joint. The plastic thread going through the limb and body is often very thick and might damage the fabric. Cotter pins, on the other hand, require only a few threads to be pushed apart. Yet the holes are seldom visible, only in those cases when the joint has been assembled on the wrong side. The best reason for not using plastic joints is that they can break with age.

The use of screws inside a bear is most unpleasant in my experience. This technique makes it necessary to handle two tools at one time: the bolt is turned with the screwdriver (spanner) while the wrench holds the nut or the other way around. In doing so, I often slipped, and there was a problem with the head: the unsecured screw rotated inside. Friedel Rowe suggests that the screw can be secured with masking tape (four pieces forming a star over the head of the screw) to stop turning. Usually, the bolts are fixed with a special glue, and there are also self-locking nuts. In any case, it's a nuisance having to turn and hold at the same time.

Another choice for jointing your teddy bears is the "pop rivet", which is unknown in Germany but rather common in the United States. Since I don't have any experience, I asked my friend Debbi Henretty to describe this method. "Although I am not sure of the history, the name can certainly be attributed to the "pop" noise made during the riveting process. The rivet takes the place of your bolt and nut. Each joint will, of course, still require two disks (one inside the limb or head; one inside the body), two washers (same positions) and a rivet. You will also need a rivet gun (rivets and rivet guns are readily available from your local hardware store).

"To joint, you will place a washer and a disk on the rivet. Insert the end of the rivet through the limb into the body. From inside the body, place a disk, then a washer on the rivet. Hold in place. Now, following the directions provided with your gun, insert the other end of the rivet into the gun and pump. When you hear the POP the joint is complete.

"The advantage to this is that the rivet provides a very strong joint and can be very tight. It is, however, more difficult to control the tightness of the joint and you may get some variation from limb to limb. You must also determine the best rivet for your application based on the thickness of the fur and the disc you are using. Another consideration is that it requires a certain amount of strength to pump the rivet gun. Over several years and several hundred bears, I found this took a toll on my hand, wrist and elbow."

I have returned to the oldest form of assembling: cardboard disks and cotter pins. During my time as a teddy doctor I noticed that this kind of joint is surprisingly durable. Even on rather battered bears the disks and pins were still in good shape.

Cardboard disks can be purchased in a huge variety of sizes. They range from $^{1}/_{2}$-inch (0.7 cm) for miniatures to 4-1/2 inches (12 cms) for big bears, their sizes increasing in small increments of about 0.2 inches (0.5 cms). Therefore, each joint can be matched with a disk of just the right size. If you like to make lots of bears, it pays to build yourself a stock of disks in different sizes. However, if you only make a bear now and then, you've probably got the time to make your own cardboard disks.

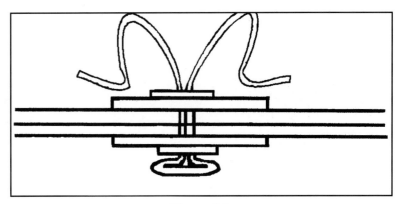

Figure 8A.

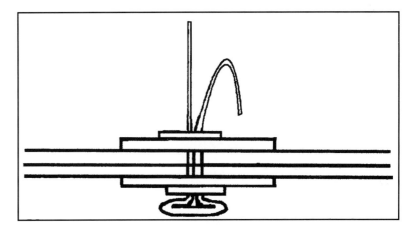

Figure 8B.

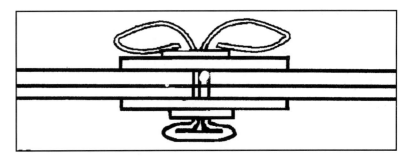

Figure 8C.

These may not be bendable, so you may have to glue several layers of cardboard together. Disks of plywood or hardboard, sawn with a hole cutter, are useful as well. Hole cutters adjust to nearly any size.

Cotter pins and washers are sold in hardware stores. Suitable washers have a size of $^{1}/_{2}$-inch (1 cm) to 0.8-inch (2 cms), with a .1-inch (.3 cm) hole. Cotter pins are available in many lengths and gauges. For a medium-sized bear, they should have a length of about 1-1/2 inches (4 cms). Some retailers offer T-shaped cotter pins, which are rather pleasant to work with.

For one joint, you'll always need two equal-sized disks, two washers and one cotter pin. For some bear makers, bending the pin is an art in itself, but don't panic. I've repaired lots of bears with their cotter pins simply twirled, yet lasting for decades. I myself don't have the grasp of these complicated cotter crowns (Fig. 8a), but I first bend the cotter pins about halfway (Fig. 8b), then press them flat against the disk (Fig. 8c). The one thing of importance is that you put some pressure to the disk to keep the joint from becoming loose. You can use ordinary tweezers (pliers) for bending. It is even more comfortable to use special cotter keys, which look like a screwdriver with a cleft. With them, you only turn and no longer have to hold the tweezers together. An advantage of cotter pin joints is that you can stuff and sew up arms and legs before assembling them to the body (Photo 2).

Swivel Heads and Swinging Joints

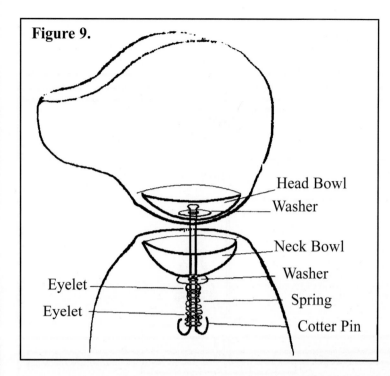

Figure 9.

Head Bowl
Washer

Neck Bowl
Washer
Spring
Cotter Pin

Eyelet
Eyelet

All the joints I mentioned before can be turned back and forth. However, you may want your bear's head to move up and down like a doll's. For this purpose, there are, at least in the United States, special metal swivel joints. I have tried them and they work well, but are rather time consuming. Since I found them too expensive for permanent use, I spent years looking for my own solutions. Here's the technique I use, which is easy and cheap. Instead of flat neck disks, I use neck bowls made out of cardboard in a number of sizes. They are designed for restoring the bodies of porcelain dolls and are available from doll supply companies. They come in many sizes, but unfortunately may be difficult to get.

The bowl is inserted into the head instead of the disk, but uses a cotter pin and washer in the same way. A second bowl is placed inside the body instead of the counter disk. Then the head is attached, with the head bowl fitting into the body bowl. The pin projects into the body through the bowl's opening. A washer is planted onto it as usual, but before the cotter pin is turned, it also gets a wire spring. Long springs are available in various diameters at the hardware store. Both ends of the spring, which I cut at a length of 0.4 inches (1 cm) to 0.8 inches (2 cms), are secured with an eyelet, then the protruding end of the cotter key is bent. This makes the head more flexible (Fig. 9).

Usually, a teddy's joints should be tight, not swinging around loosely. However, you may like to make a teddy baby with loose joints and a wobbly head. Again, cotter pins and disks are required. But this time, the pin is inserted into the neck disk not with the ends, but with the curve (don't use T-shaped cotter keys!) projecting out of the head. A second cotter pin is hooked into this loop and then secured inside the body in the normal way (Fig. 10). This will result in a swinging neck joint that nevertheless holds fast.

After inserting the neck disk (or bowl), it's best to close the neck opening with a long, straight seam using a ladder stitch (Fig.11a). The seam should not be gathered around the opening and pulled, because this will result in an uneven surface. Since this area is stressed each time the

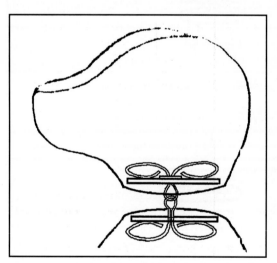

Figure 10.

teddy's head is moved, it's better to work with as little friction as possible. Many bears with head openings that were only pulled together in the factory either get a slack head or loose it.

For closing the head and the other openings, you will need a thin thread that is stronger than the yarn used for sewing bears. With a ladder stitch, you always tear both sides of the opening together and the sewing yarn would break. Bear suppliers offer a special polyester thread in various colors, which works very well.

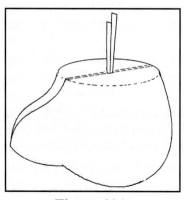

Figure 11A.

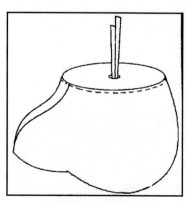

Figure 11B.

Bendable Arms

If you are using cotter pin joints, you may finish the arms and legs before assembling them. Otherwise, the limbs are assembled first, then stuffed.

Arms and legs become extra posable when you insert a bendable inlay before stuffing. Moveable plastic inlays, or "Flexlimb"®, are available for this purpose. However, self-made wire inlays are cheaper. You can use sisal-coated wire, bending the ends so the wire won't poke through and mantling them with insulating tape or sticking plaster. I prefer working with the foam-coated wire, "Florifix"®, which is actually intended to tie trees. It comes in 10-meter rolls. Flexible soft hair curlers are also suitable, but more expensive. I pinch off the wire at the length of the arm and bend the ends. For larger bears, I double the wire and twist it. This way, I get a solid, yet bendable inlay. The wire is then loosely inserted into the arm and stuffing carefully added around it. Take care not to stuff too much, as this robs the arm of its bendability. Of course, this would not work with wood-wool, which always has to be stuffed tightly. Otherwise, it's nice if the bear can bend its arms to hold an object.

Figure 12.

For a contest, my daughter Maja wanted to make bears that could spread their arms away from their bodies. She created this effect by leaving out the arm disks and putting the arm wire straight through the body, going from one paw to the other. She didn't change the pattern and stitched the arms to the body. At first glance, the bears look like ordinary teddies, but are totally free in their arm movements (Figure 12 and Photo 58).

No-No-Bears

Figure 13.

Since the 1930s, teddy bears that can move their heads up and down as if nodding or turn them left and right by a head-and-tail-mechanism have been very popular. They are called "yes-no-bears". The mechanisms can be purchased (from the *Edinburgh* Company) and inserted using the manufacturer's instructions.

A no-no-mechanism, which allows a bear to shake its head by moving its tail, can easily be constructed using simple means. I use a thick wire, such as those used to tighten wire fences. First, I bend a loop fitting the muzzle and stuff carefully around it so it can't be felt from the outside. Then, the head gets the usual disk and is sewn up. The long piece of wire projecting out of the head is inserted into the body, and I secure the counter disk with a plastic locker like those used for plastic joints. The wire then leaves the body at the posterior and is bent into a small loop as well. After stuffing the bear as usual, I sew a suitable tail, which is then pulled over the loop and sewn to the body (Fig. 13).

Mounting

On most teddy patterns, the areas to attach the arms and legs are already marked. If you'd like to design your own pattern, you'll need to determine placement by yourself. I usually don't mark it on the pattern, but on the bear itself. First, the head is fixed. If the body consists of four parts or has a dart at the top, the joint enters close to the seams' crossing. If it has a two-part body, mount the head either in the upper middle or barely in front of it (Fig. 14). If you mount the head too far to the back, the bear will gaze skyward for the rest of its life, which looks even worse than if it were looking down. Teddies with a large hump must have their heads mounted in front of it, never upon the hump!

The legs are assembled in the area of the side seam or where it would be. Lay the body out flat, with the belly and back seam forming the edges. The point of attachment must be halfway between the tummy and the back; otherwise the bear will have trouble sitting and standing. Place the leg's counter disk on the real or supposed flank line. Depending on the teddy's size, keep some distance from the bottom to the lower edge, i.e. the crotch. For an 11-inch (28 cm) bear, this would be about a finger's width, with more space for larger bears and less for smaller ones (Fig. 15). If the legs are mounted too low, the teddy will be sitting on its legs and tend to stand cross-legged (Fig. 16). On the other hand, legs that are too high will make it stand straddle-legged and wobble in the sitting position (Fig. 17). If both sides of the body are facing exactly against each other, you can pierce both layers at one time to mark the point of the leg attachments. The hole in the disk marks the right place.

The arms are also mounted along the real or imagined side seam, but not in the seam that could easily open. Lay the arm disk onto this line and keep some distance from the base of the head. If the arms are attached too high, the bear will shrug its shoulders permanently (Fig. 16), which looks worse than arms sitting too low (Fig. 17), since they are also sticking out. The arms will also stick out if they are mounted too close to the back.

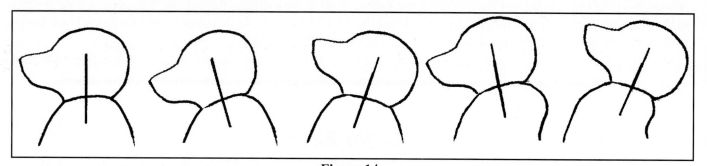

Figure 14.

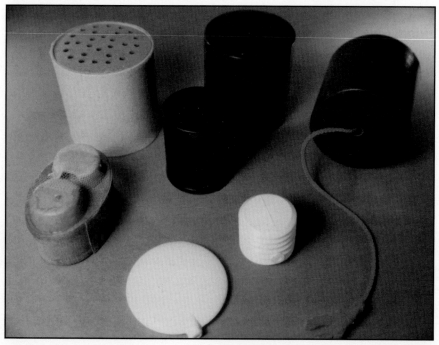

4. Various bear voices. The growlers pictured in the back row come in different sizes and may be made of cardboard as well as plastic. The voice on the right is a growler as well, but it works by pulling instead of turning. This type was used for the large riding bears. Pressing voices have a very different sound – the bear will not growl, but squeak. They are inserted towards the tummy of the bear. If used often, the bear may lose his hair in the area where the voice must be pressed. The traditional shape (left) produces two tones. The modern plastic voices make rather high squeaks and are usually used for toys rather than artist bears. *Photograph by Lars Wege.*

After mounting, stuff the arms and legs, or, if they are already finished, stuff only the body. It is important to keep an eye on the crucial parts, like the tips of the feet. Beginners tend not to stuff them full enough. Inside the body, pay close attention to the areas between the joints as well as the shoulders and tummy. You'll probably need a tool to get the filling distributed everywhere. Check the body carefully before closing the back seam.

If your teddy is to get a growler, it should be inserted when the tummy is stuffed but the back is not (Fig.18). To prevent the filling from entering the holes of the growler, you should place it into a small bag, such as one made of old nylons. Stuff around the growler and pad it at the back. The air holes pointing back or forth decide whether your bear growls when turned over forward or backward.

Like the openings on the arms and legs, close the back by using a ladder stitch. If you work carefully, since the edges are being drawn together the thread should be invisible afterwards.

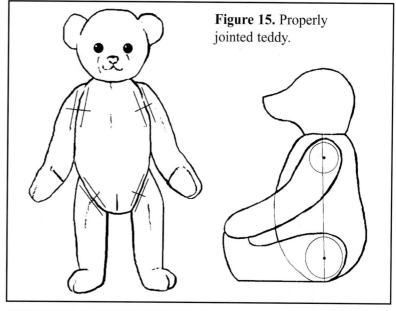

Figure 15. Properly jointed teddy.

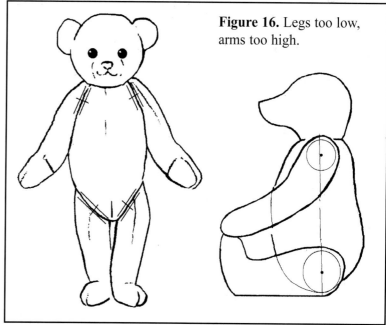

Figure 16. Legs too low, arms too high.

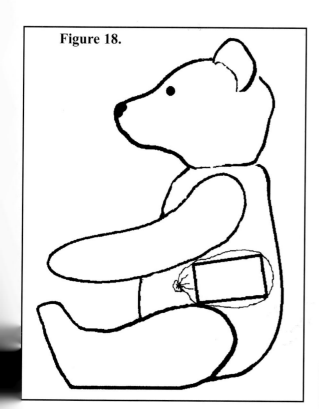

Figure 18.

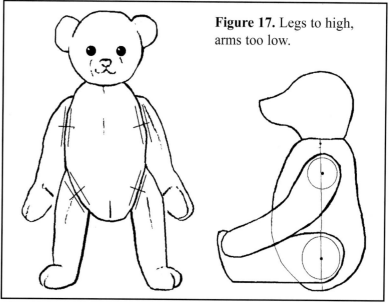

Figure 17. Legs to high, arms too low.

17

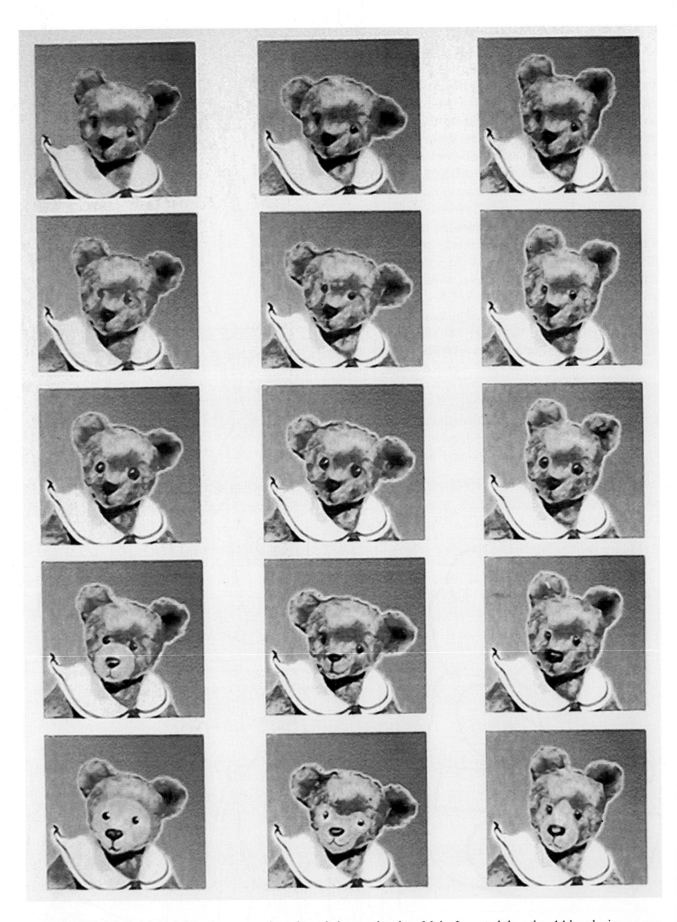

5. Only the first bear on the left in the top row is real, made by my daughter Maja. I created the other 14 by playing on my computer. I changed the size and placement of the eyes, the ears, and the nose to show just how different bears made of the same pattern can look. There are many more possibilities than I can show on this page.

The Face

Now here's your bear, without eyes, ears or nose. The work which follows is the most interesting in all bear making, as you might imagine, for it will determine your teddy's character. Unfortunately, this is also the domain where most mistakes are made and even a well-sewn bear can be spoiled.

To illustrate this, I used transparent paper to trace the head of a bear I saw in a teddy magazine. In my opinion, he looked rather unhappy. The second drawing of the bear with changed eyes and nose shows a far more contented expression (Fig. 19).

Figure 19.

6. Two of my early bears from bought patterns, made of llama, 12 and 16 inches (31 and 41 cm). Both teddies have inserted ears that are too far in front of the head. The nose of the white teddy is embroidered rather low, and her mouth is very small for a bear of her size. In addition, the brown glass eyes look red on the white fabric.

7. Early bears from bought patterns. The left teddy was made from the same pattern as the white one and features the same ear problems. Both bears have rather large eyes, which are not pulled in enough, and their noses are embroidered very low. The ears of the right teddy are inserted at the middle of the head (compare Fig. 21) his arms are very short.

19

8. "Tünnes" was one of my early bears made from real fur following a bought pattern. Because of problems sewing the fur, his ears have rather bad placement (left), but wearing his cap gives him quite a nice expression (right).

Left and Above:

9. "Xaver" was one of my first bears. He is made of cotton plush and shows some of the typical mistakes made by beginners. His nose is embroidered very low and the ears are placed badly. His brown glass eyes look red on the yellow fabric. But "Xaver" seems to be very content wearing his "lederhosen", hat and glasses.

10. "Dieter" (on the left) was made of sheepskin a year after "Xaver." I think his big ears are placed too far in the middle of his head. I moved the ears back in the picture on the right using a computer trick so you can see the difference.

11. A woman in my bear making class did not like the bear she had made at home, which is shown in the left photographs. The main problem is that the nose and mouth were embroidered very low, making the teddy look a bit rat-like. The ears are also placed too far in the middle of the head, but were not changed. My client decided to remove the old nose and embroider it again. The teddy bear looked much better afterwards, as shown in the right photographs.

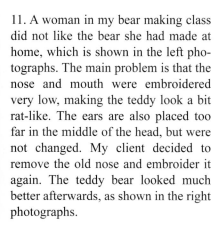

12. A young woman brought me some bears that she had made from kits by herself. Since she had no instruction, she made nearly every mistake that was possible. So I spent the whole afternoon giving her advice. The bear features eyes sewn on like buttons. Since she did not know how to embroider the mouth, she had left it off. My client had also noticed that something was wrong with the arms. The right one was jointed properly, but she did not find the proper place for the left, so it was attached at the center seam of the body. The bear looks quite nice after some arm surgery, the addition of an embroidered mouth and having his pop-eyes pulled in.

Bottom photos:
A bear maker who had bought the German version of my book sent me some photographs of her bears. Compare the original photo on the left with the right one. I have altered by computer to show how only slight changes concerning the place of arms and nose will improve this little guy.

Ears

Figure 20.

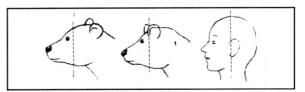

Figure 21.

In the beginning, I pointed out that it's better to attach the ears afterwards. The drawing shows you how different the same bear would look with the ears in another position (Fig. 20).

Place pins (the longer, the better) through the edges of the sewn-up ears and try them out to see which position you like best (Fig 23). Remember that both ears are symmetrical, so you also need to inspect the bear from above. Then view him from the side. Concerning the ears, there's a great difference between bears and humans. Human ears are placed right in the center when viewed in profile, while bears' ears sit rather in the back. If you want your teddy to look bear-like, pay attention to this point (Fig. 21).

The height and size of the ears varies for real bears as well (Fig. 22). For example, polar bears have very small ears, placed on the sides of the head, while black bears' ears are far larger and placed higher up. Of course, no real bears have their ears sitting on the cheek, like Merrythought's "Cheeky".

Bear's ears are never flat, but curved like a shell. This looks good on teddies, too, so don't pin the ears to the head stretched out, but in a semicircle curving forward

(Fig. 23). Being right-handed, I start with the right ear, muzzle pointing towards me. I insert the needle (no matter where) and come out at the lower corner of the ear. After attaching the thread, I secure this corner to the head with a couple of stitches. Then I sew on the back side of the ear (ladder stitch, of course, alternating stitches into ear and head). I place my left thumb into the center of the ear in order to achieve a well-shaped curve. The ear-corner at the center of the head is sewn tightly to the head, as well. To sew along the inner ear, I can flap the ear back slightly without having the curve disappear. As a precaution, I sew twice around the ears, being well aware of their uses as teddy's handle. For the left ear, I start with the corner pointing towards the center and sew the back side first.

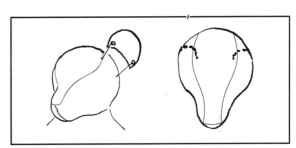

Figure 23.

Figure 22.

Brown Bear.

Polar Bear.

American Black Bear.

Spectacled Bear.

Asiatic Black Bear.

Panda.

Sun Bear.

Sloth Bear.

Trimming

If you're not working with a short-pile material like cotton plush or camel hair, your bear should be shaved now. In my experience, beginners tend to shrink from this because they are afraid of cutting off too much of the expensive hairs. Some people prefer unshaved bears, as well. Although I approve of men with beards, I think of unshaved bears as somewhat unfinished.

Looking at real bears, you'll find that they have hardly any hair on their snouts, even if the rest of their fur is thick and shaggy. You can easily guess the reason why if you imagine the bear gutting a stag. Your teddy won't do that, of course, but its muzzle will simply show off better with short hair. On unshaved bears, the features of the face seem blurred. Some bear makers shave only the upper part of the nose and leave a walrus moustache, which gives the bear a dog-like look.

Afraid to cut off too much, beginners often trim only a small area around the nose, which usually looks unconvincing. If you're not certain, tie a string around the muzzle up to the place where the head turns rounder and shave in this area. To shave, I like to use my husband's beard-trimmer, but a pair of scissors also works.

If you take a look at bears made by professionals, you'll hardly ever find untrimmed ones. They are more common with manufactured bears. since trimming requires an extra process. The type of trimming is a sign of the bear maker's personal style. Often, the form of the snout is especially striking because only short stubble remains.

The method of shaving you chose depends on your own taste and the type of bear. There's the dispersing shave, with the hair turning longer gradually in the transition between the muzzle and the rest of the head, or the sharp shave with a clear dividing line. You may also shave beyond the muzzle. There are suggestions in Figure 50.

Eyes

The eyes determine if and how a bear looks at people. The first problem occurs with the proper choice of eyes. If you're not making a bear for a baby or toddler, thus using security eyes, you should chose glass eyes. Plastic eyes on a loop not only look bad, but are also easily scratched.

Beginners often use brown glass eyes, while most professionals use black ones. Brown glass eyes look reddish on a bear, especially if the fur is light-colored (Photo 6). With transparent glass eyes, you also have to pay close attention to both pupils being of equal size. Larger pupils give the bear a friendlier look than very small ones, which make the bear look rather menacing.

Besides brown glass eyes, there are also blue ones and colorless ones with a black pupil. The latter can be painted on the back with a covering paint in the color you desire.

Black glass eyes usually look livelier than light ones. Although they are completely black, on the finished bear they create the effect of a dark eye with a black pupil.

Glass eyes are available with loops or as pairs on wire, which are usually less expensive. You can make the loops yourself by cutting the wire 1 or $^1/_2$ inches (1 to 3 cms) and bending it. When using these eyes, be careful that they have the same size - sometimes the eyes on one wire are different.

There's no standard rule for the size of the eyes, either. Real bears have relatively small eyes. A teddy looks more bear-like and more grown-up the smaller the eyes are. Larger eyes make it look more childish and friendly. But look out! If the eyes are too big it will make your bear look ugly (Fig. 24).

Black glass eyes are available in all sizes with a diameter from 0.03-inch (.1 cm) to $^3/_4$-inch (2 cm). If you'd like to make lots of bears, you'd better build a stock of eyes in various sizes and find the right size by holding the different eyes up to the bear. If you seldom make bears, don't be afraid of taking the bear to a hobby shop and finding the right size there. Unfortunately, many shops have a poor assortment of eyes; many stock only brown ones in a few sizes. Brown eyes may be painted on the back with black paint to make them look better.

Many beginners have trouble finding the right placement for the eyes. There are lots of ways, of course, but the eyes should never be placed onto the forehead, as is often done. The right place is usually at the end of the muzzle where it develops into the forehead. If your pattern has a gusset, this often widens in the area of the eyes. Real grown-up bears have rather narrow-set eyes, while cubs' eyes are wider apart and larger, but never in the area of the nose (Fig. 25).

13. Various types of eyes. Left: glass eyes with loops; Center: glass eyes on wires; Right: plastic security eyes. *Photograph by Lars Wege.*

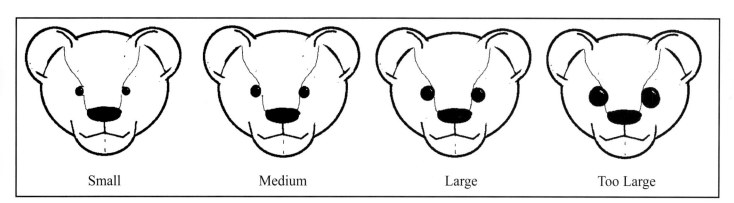

Small   Medium   Large   Too Large

Figure 24.

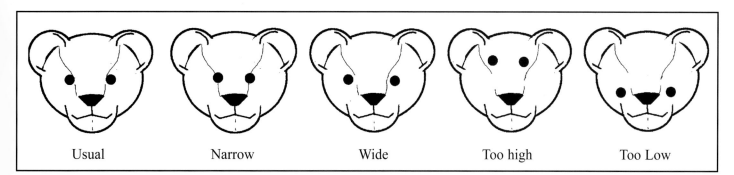

Usual   Narrow   Wide   Too high   Too Low

Figure 25.

Before inserting the eyes, you need to be sure that they are both of the same size. Sometimes, the size varies even for a pair of eyes on the same wire. With colored eyes, the pupils must match as well. Test the placement of the eyes by using colored pins and holding the eyes up to the head.

A better option: if you can find eyes on wire instead of loops, create pairs in different sizes by cutting the wire at a length of $^1/_2$ to 1 inch (1 to 3 cms). You can use these eyes instead of pins, and they will give you a better idea of how the eyes will look. Sets for this purpose "true eyes" are available too.

Once you've made up your mind about placement, thread a long piece of eye thread through your long eye needle. Make sure the needle is long enough, approximately 4 inches (10 cms), but also has an opening wide enough – otherwise you cannot string the eye thread. If you cannot find the right needle in your hobby shop, you may be more successful at an upholsterer's, where you're most likely to find long upholstery needles of 6 to 8 inches (15 to 20 cms) as well, which are needed for making huge bears.

A special eye thread is available at suppliers. If you can't get eye thread, you may use pearl embroidery floss in a matching color, thin fishing line, or dental floss. The very best thread I know for inserting the eyes is artificial sinew. It comes in thick rolls and may be used for very large bears as well as for miniatures, since you can divide the sinew into threads as thin as needed. I've never managed to tear even the very thin strands I use for miniatures. One roll will last for a long time. I got one two years ago, and since I usually make rather small bears I have not used half of it.

Never sew a bear's eyes to the head like buttons, which will give the bear pop-eyes (Photo 12). If you purchased the eyes on a wire, cut the wire off about $^1/_2$-inch (1 to 2 cms) near the eye and form a loop of the short end. Don't simply stick the wire into the head, this is only for experimenting. Insert your needle and thread into the bear's head in the marked spot, then exit the opposite side of the head right behind the ear. Now both ends of your thread stick out of the head. String the eye on the thread in front and insert this same thread into the needle again. Push it into the same hole, this time coming out a finger's width next to the first point (Fig. 26). With the two ends of the thread hanging out of the head, you can pull the eye right into the head, causing the loop to vanish inside (Fig. 27). You may have to tweak the loop together to help it slip into the hole. Sometimes you will make the hole a little bit wider.

After inserting the second eye the same way, take another critical look to see whether it is in the right place and is the right size. If everything is all right, fasten the eyes. Pull both ends of the string tight, forming a slight depression around the eye. This "eye socket" gives the bear a livelier look than if the eyes were resting flat upon the face. You can easily test this effect while inserting your bear's eyes.

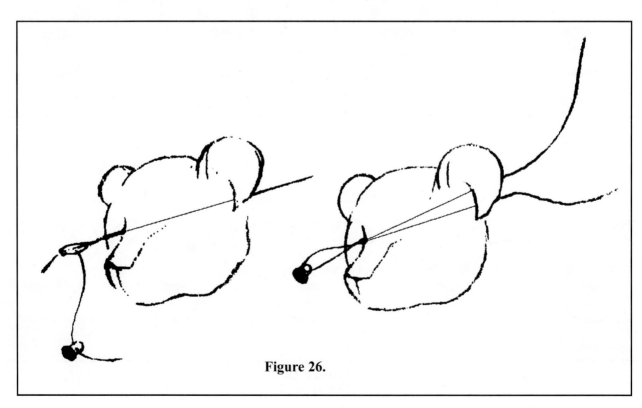

Figure 26.

To keep the knot from loosening during the process, make a surgical knot instead of a common double knot (Fig. 28). You'll need to loop the thread around not once, but twice. After tying, draw the threads into the head right next to the knot and pull them out anywhere. Then pull the thread tight and cut it right above the surface. Safety eyes are plastic eyes with a shank that must be pushed through the fabric and secured with a plastic or metal washer. This is done before stuffing the head, making it harder to find the right place. The safest, but most time consuming, way is to stuff the head, mark the position of the eye and take the stuffing out again.

One disadvantage of these eyes is that they cannot be drawn into the head, but rest flat against the face. To create an eye socket, you can draw an eye thread through the head right next to the security eye, yet this time not stitching twice into the same hole, but close beside it. Then pull both ends of the thread tight and make a knot in the neck or behind the eye.

If you think that the safety eyes are not in the right place after finishing your bear, you don't have to take off the head. Just open the seam a little near the eyes, wide enough to remove the washer. Then, you can move the eyes without having to disassemble everything. The procedure is the same, of course, if an eye breaks, for even safety eyes may do so.

If an old or new bear needs extra stuffing, you can also simply open a seam a bit. With the aid of a hemostat, the new filling is taken to the right place. Afterwards, the open seam is sewn up with a ladder stitch as invisibly as possible.

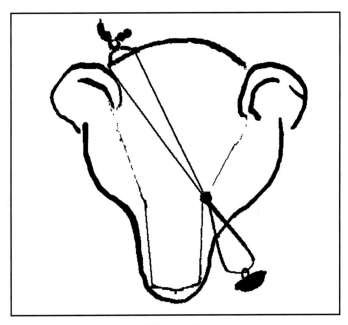

Figure 27.

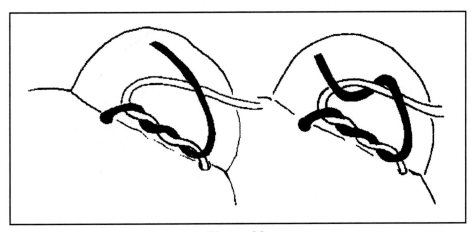

Figure 28.

Nose

Figure 29.

Now your bear is looking at you, but an important part of the face is still missing: the nose and mouth. Please don't get the idea of letting it have a plastic nose – you don't want it to look like a cheap carnival bear! My daughter Maja found it very difficult to embroider noses in the beginning and would rather stitch on a piece of cloth. The result was not very pretty, of course, so she trained in embroidering. Now her bears have very well stitched noses. You too should not let yourself be discouraged, but take some time, as you can tell a good bear by its beautifully stitched nose. Maybe you'll regard bears by professionals under this aspect. They usually have very well stitched noses, which in their various shapes often bear the personal "signature" of the bear maker (Fig. 29).

You may feel uncertain about the size of the nose and the place where it's going to be. Cut a nose (or several) out of black felt and pin it to a spot you think is suitable. Then you can decide if the size and form please you, but the most important task is to find the right spot. Many mistakes are made at this point. A bear's nose belongs in the spot where the nose line bends. If your pattern has a gusset down to the tip of the nose, one part of the nose goes on this gusset above the seam, the other part below. Often the nose is stitched too low, and the mouth automatically turns out too low as well (Fig. 30). Noses that are stitched too high are less annoying if the snout is not too short.

The shape and size of the nose may vary and depends on your personal taste. Look at as many teddies as possible and compare their noses. Generally, a bear with a large nose will look more bearish and grown up, while a small nose results in a childish or lady-like look. As a beginner, you should avoid extremes in both directions.

Once you've found the right spot and decided on the shape, you can thread your needle, which should be an embroidery needle with a sharp point. Usually perle cotton yarn is used, but you can also use embroidery floss. You'll get the best results with a thin thread, even though the work takes a little longer.

Insert your needle somewhere around the muzzle and pull it out in the area of the nose. Anchor the thread tightly, then cut off the loose end. Next, stitch an outline in the size and shape of the nose in three or four long stitches from one end to the other (Fig. 31a). Either remove the felt or leave it underneath the nose. Sometimes it works well to shave off all the hair in the area of the nose.

Then, using a satin stitch, fill in the outline (Fig. 31b). It's better to stitch the nose in two layers, which makes it look more pronounced and no "skin" shows through (Fig. 31c). You can of course use thicker yarn for the lower layer. Fill in the outlined area with dense horizontal stitches. Then stitch a second layer in thin yarn with vertical stitches. Work accurately; the threads should lay straight, one next to the other. Take care at the edges to avoid a messy outline. I myself use a magnifier lamp when stitching the nose. If the upper edge of the nose is not straight, you can adjust this with a black textile pen, thus, minor mistakes can be hidden. You can also use the textile pen to paint single unshaved hairs protruding out of the nose in black, or you can try to pull out the odd hair with a pair of tweezers or a hemostat.

If the thread seems to be loose although you worked carefully, it's most likely that the snout is lacking stuffing. In this case, open the neck seam and insert a little more stuffing. It's hard to stitch on a nose that is too soft.

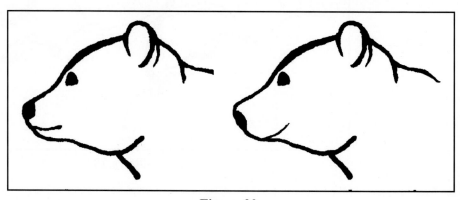

Figure 30.

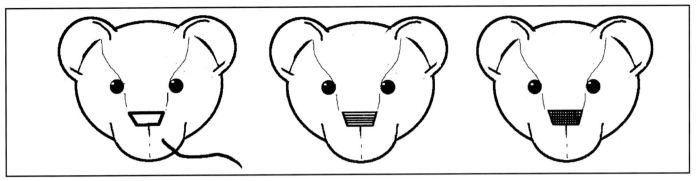

Figure 31A.   **Figure 31B.**   **Figure 31C.**

Mouth

It is possible to try out the teddy's mouth first, as well. There are a number of possibilities, which determine the facial expression of your bear (Fig. 32). My daughter Maja tests the shape of the mouth in this way: she marks the corner points of the mouth with pins and wraps the thread around them. Then she is able to see the appearance of the mouth without stitching and, by moving the pins, she can correct the shape without having to unwrap the thread. Once she's decided on the right shape, she removes the thread and stitches from pin to pin (Fig. 33). This procedure works well to aid in stitching the mouth symmetrically, and the effect is easy to see. Beginners especially tend to stitch the mouth too small. My first bear, "Lieschen", is a typical pointed nose bear. Remember that the mouth of a bear looks more like that of a beast of prey, not like a human mouth at all. This means that the stitched mouth should be visible in profile too, and must not be only in the front area of the muzzle. In addition, the mouth should not be stitched too low. The lower jaw of a bear is nearly as long as the muzzle, so if you place the mouth too low, the bear gets a rat-like face (Figures 30 and 34 and Photo 11, left).

Most teddies' noses are black, but of course you may use any other color as well if it suits your bear. Bear cubs are born with pink noses, by the way, but they have turned to black by the time the cub leaves the cave for the first time.

To create the effect of early sealing-wax noses, you can dab the nose with liquid wax, which gives it a compact surface. It is helpful to use a hair dryer after applying the wax to get it into the thread. Some bear makers also use varnish to get a special effect on the nose.

As a finishing touch, brush out the seams. There are special brushes with small hooks for this purpose, not unlike the type of brush used for dogs. It's very easy to brush out the seams with a brush like this and it also improves the appearance of hand-finished seams by making them look more or less invisible. If you don't have a brush, you can also pick the hairs out of the seams with the help of a needle. The brushing is most important on the ears, which don't look fluffy unless the hair is standing up. For the paws too, it looks better if the hair is carefully teased out at the seams.

You will have noticed my attention to detail again and again. This is because I've heard slipshod work too often excused with, "Well, it's handmade, you see?" One should expect accuracy from handicraft most of all.

On the other hand, remember that it is not perfection alone that determines a teddy's quality. The special expression and the personality are most important. A friend of mine put it this way, "The bear has got to look at me and call my name."

Figure 32.

Figure 33.

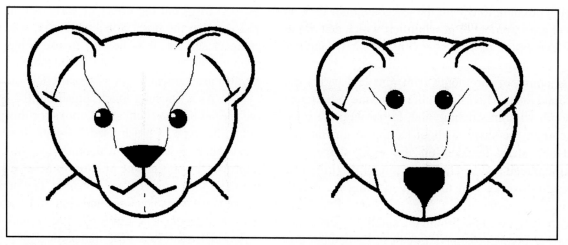

Figure 34. The bear on the right shows three faults, which are very often combined: the eyes are placed on the forehead, the nose and mouth are embroidered too low, and the ears come too close to the face.

Variations

Your teddy is finished. How do you like him? Surely he is not going to remain alone. However, you don't want to make a number of clones of this bear. You can alter his appearance by using different fabrics with longer or shorter pile. Then he will always look different.

You also can make your bear in different sizes. Use the Kombi pattern you will find in the appendix of this book. You can enlarge or reduce it with the aid of a copy machine. If you have a computer with a scanner, this will work perfectly too. We have done it with this pattern and have produced very different bears in sizes from 16 inches (41 cms) down to 2 inches (5 cms) and less. The original size is 10 inches (25 cms), but since the design is very classic it looked good in any size (Photos 111 - 119).

Big Bears

You should not enlarge any patterns to make huge bears, especially over 18 inches (46 cms). Childlike, cuddly bears are cute in a size of 9 inches (23 cms), but blown up to 18, they seem plump (Photo 60). The head will be too big and the arms may be too short. Instead, choose the classical designs for large bears. I will explain more about the differences in the chapter, "Proportions." Perhaps you should reduce the head and not use the same magnification as the rest of the body. Before cutting the fur, try laying your pattern pieces out to get an idea of the proportions. Apart from the size of the head, make sure that the arms are long enough. Look at pictures of old Steiff bears: their proportions harmonize even at a size of 30 inches (76 cms), while large fairground bears seem stout and plump.

If you want to make a huge bear, you may not be able to purchase disks of the right sizes, so it's best to cut them out yourself from plywood. If your bear is very large, use thick screws or very large cotter pins. Huge bears also consume lots of filling. If you'd like to save money, you can fill the belly with (clean) old pullovers and such. As large bears also tend to grow very heavy, wood-wool can be used to make them lightweight.

Another problem may be getting eyes in the proper size. Lesch, the biggest company for animal and dolls eyes in Germany, offers a diameter up to 1-$\frac{1}{4}$-inch (30 mm) in plastic and 1-inch (25 mm) in glass. If you can't find eyes, use black buttons instead.

You will also use a lot of fabric, of course, which may be very expensive. Plan a big bear very thoughtfully to avoid disappointments.

Left: (two photos)
14. Two large bears, typical for fairgrounds. They feature large heads and trunks, short straight arms, and very small feet.

15. Friedel Rowe's bears look well proportioned even being 35.5 inches (90 cm) tall like "Max", as they feature a very classic style.

Small Bears and Miniatures

16. Mini bear by Anna Ilisch. Upholstery plush, 2-1/4 inches (6 cm). *Photograph by Lars Wege.*

For making miniatures we have not only made special designs, but also downsized many of our patterns with good results. Downsizing a pattern is less difficult than enlarging. You can take any good pattern you have designed and reduce it, or you may use the patterns you find in this book. We have made small bears using my daughter Maja's Kombi pattern in 8 inches (20 cms), 6 inches (15 cms), 4 inches (10 cms) and 2 inches (5 cms). They all turned out well (Photographs 116 - 119).

You can use different fabrics for making small bears, but the smaller the bear is, the shorter the pile should be. I have tried mohair, camel hair and cotton plush for bears as small as 3 inches (8 cms). If you have enough scraps to make a small bear but you feel the pile is too long - no problem, you can shave it as you like. I prefer upholstery plush to make miniature bears because it is very difficult to turn the tiny pieces if they are made of a thicker fabric. Usually, the ears are the tiniest pieces of your pattern. Make sure you will be able to turn them when choosing the fabric.

Upholstery plush is usually sold in small pieces, 10-inch (25 cm) squares for example. This is enough to make several miniatures. The plush comes in many colors, and the pile may be shiny or dull and its length can be varied. It is rather hard to get long-piled upholstery plush, which is more expensive as well.

The quality may be different, too. Some plush tends to tear more easily than others will. With all types you must sew very carefully, especially when you close the back. Don't stuff too hard, and do all the stuffing and sewing with a lot of "feeling" to avoid damaging the fabric.

17. Mini bear by Anna Ilisch. Upholstery plush, 2-1/4 inches (6 cm). *Photograph by Lars Wege.*

For miniatures, you will need tools for turning and stuffing. I have bought special tools for turning, but could not manage to use them. I prefer my hemostat. Some suppliers sell very tiny ones, which are very good for miniatures. I also use a pair of tweezers with thin, but not sharp, ends for turning and stuffing. Other colleagues use toothpicks while stuffing.

You can use fiberfill, unspun wool or kapok as stuffing material. To make the teddies heavier, very tiny glass beads may be used, but be sure they do not contain lead.

18. Mini bears, 2-1/2 inches (6 cm).

19. "Ruby" by Anna Ilisch, 2 inches (5 cm).

20. 2-1/2-inch (6 cm) mini bear.

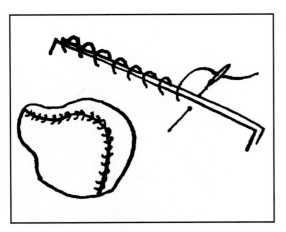

Figure 35.

Many bear makers sew small bears by hand. This is not a problem, since the seams are not very long. Especially for miniatures, many bear makers cut out the pieces without a seam allowance and sew by using a "whipstitch"(Fig. 35). This stitch is easy and fast to do, but since the upholstery plush tends to be damaged easily, you must be careful not to make too many stitches, but on the other hand, be sure you make enough. Most of the time, the seam will to be visible after turning and stuffing. I prefer sewing minis with a small seam allowance using the double running stitch (Fig. 4c) or the quite common backstitch (Fig. 4b). With these stitches, you won't see the seams afterwards and the bear looks tidier.

I am a little bit lazy, so I prefer to sew even my minis by machine. My sewing machine has different "feet", and two of them have small "windows" through which I can see the drawn line while sewing (Fig. 36). You might find them listed as "quilting foot" or "little foot."

As I mentioned in the chapter about sewing, I sew tiny parts before cutting them out. In tiny teddies, you can reduce the body to two parts and leave out the darts, so sewing before cutting is no problem. The same is true with the legs, but how do you sew the tiny paws by machine? It is easy, if you use this trick: I sew a stripe of the paw material in a straight line onto the fabric, then draw the pattern on both parts. Next, I cut around this piece and sew it, right sides together, onto another piece of fabric and cut it out afterwards (Fig. 37). I will sew the head by hand since it usually has a gusset or darts, and of course I sew the soles by hand as well.

For jointing the small bears, you can follow the same method as usual, using very small cotter pins and disks (Fig. 39). You may have problems finding these materials, but there are many very cheap and easy ways to joint bears of 6 inches (15 cms) and under. For the head-joint, you can use a washer and a paper

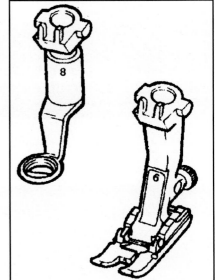

Figure 36.

fastener (butterfly pin) instead of a cotter pin (Fig. 40). This works for bears between 3 and 6 inches (8 – 15 cms). If your teddy is smaller, you can use the two parts of a metal press snap fastener as a disk. You can enlarge the hole in the middle with a nail so you can insert the cotter pin.

You can also use ordinary buttons as joints. There are different methods, but the joints for the body can easily be made from buttons. After attaching the head, the body will be stuffed firmly and

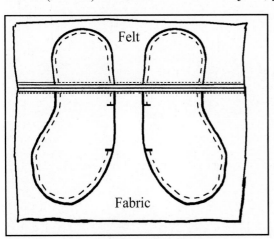

Felt

Fabric

Figure 37.

closed. Then, take four old buttons in the correct size to serve as disks for the arms and legs. You'll need a strong thread like the one used for inserting the eyes. Draw it through two holes of the button, then pull both ends through the eye of a needle. Stick the needle in the inside of the arm or leg, and when it comes out, the button will be on the inside (Fig. 38). Push the needle through the stuffed body and go from the outside into the second arm or leg. Then, remove the needle and place another button on the strings. Pull the threads and fix them with a tie (Fig. 41). This method does not work for the head joint, because it would be too loose.

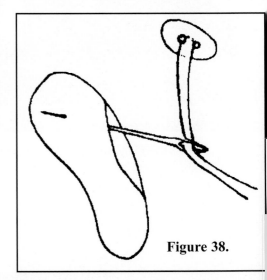

Figure 38.

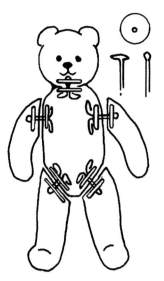

Figure 39. Discs and cotter pins for each size down to 1-1/2 inches (4 cms).

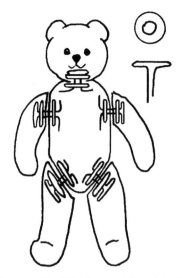

Figure 40. Washer with wide hole and paper fastener for small bears from 3 to 6 inches (8 to 15 cms).

Figure 41. Button with thread for small bears from 6 inches to miniatures. May be used with stuffed body only. No head joint.

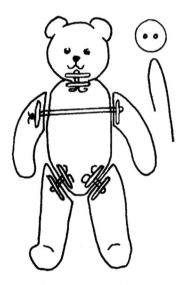

Figure 42. Button with gauge wire for small bears from 6 inches (15 cms) to miniatures. May also be used with stuffed body.

Figure 43. Self-made disc with headpin for miniatures 2 inches (5 cms) and under. May also be used with stuffed bod

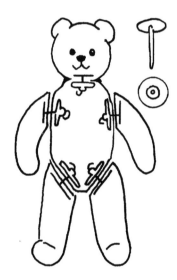

Figure 44. Earring posts with their washers for small bears from 2-1/2 to 4 inches (6 to 10 cms).

You also can use thin (22-gauge) wire instead of thread. When using this wire, you can use buttons as disks, replacing the cotter pins with the wire. Tracy Main described this method in *Teddy Bear and friends Magazine* and it also works for the head joint (Fig. 42).

For miniatures, you will need very small buttons like those used for doll clothes. If you can't find them you can make them yourself. Debbie Kessling suggests punching small disks out of plastic material such as margarine tub lids. You can insert one or two holes as required.

When using these disks with one hole, Debbie uses headpins that can easily be bent instead of cotter pins (Fig. 43). This method was used on a larger scale - hardboard disks with ordinary nails instead of cotter pins - for

a long time by several teddy bear factories in Germany. The headpins as well as the gauge-wire may also be used in the same way as the method with buttons and thread that I have described.

Another option comes from Shirley Miller. She uses both parts of earring posts that come in various sizes. I have also tried this, bending the pin after inserting the disk so it could not slip out again (Fig. 44). Since the washers usually have the same size (10 mm), this method does not work with very tiny teddies; the washers inside would be too large. I have tried to combine small earring posts with self-made disks, but found that they slipped out.

Figure 45. String joints for miniatures.

Some bear makers use a method called "thread-jointing" in miniatures. This involves attaching the arms with a stitch outside and not using any disks inside (Fig. 45). However, this causes small dents in the arms and legs and does not work with the head.

My daughter, Anna, learned to stitch on both parts of a press button on the stuffed head and body, but the result did not look very nice and sometimes the head fell off.

The face can be finished in the same way as with larger bears. Of course, you should use tiny pins when fixing the ears to the head. If you can't find tiny glass eyes, which come as small as 1/8-inch (1 mm) you can use small black pearls instead, which can be inserted in the same way as glass eyes. Pearls look better when you mark the point where they will be inserted with a fine black marker. I also paint the string around the pearl before pulling it inside to make it more or less invisible.

You should use a very thin thread for embroidering the nose and mouth. I prefer using my lamp-magnifier for this part of the work and I am very careful. It is not possible to stitch the nose again and again, since the thin fabric is easily damaged. It is not enough for a well-done miniature to be only small - it should be cute too.

Don't start with the tiniest bears. Come down step by step. To get used to small bears, I have included two very easy-to-make patterns for dollhouse bears in this book. They have only four joints and no paws (Photographs 105 - 107).

The 6-inch (15 cm) bear's body has only two pieces. Cut them out and sew the darts up, then sew both parts together with one long seam. If you sew by machine, mark the arms, legs and ears on your fabric and cut them out after sewing.

Although the 3-inch (8 cm) bear is smaller, it is also easy to make. The ears are already included. Draw the body pattern on your fabric and sew before cutting if you want to use your machine, leaving an opening in the tummy. Draw the pattern onto the other side of your fabric and pin it (right sides together) onto another piece of fabric. You can sew along the drawing line and then cut out the body. You can separate the ears with a seam after turning and before stuffing.

Each time you are successful in making a very good small bear, downsize him and try again. But don't be afraid: making miniatures is not very difficult.

One advantage of small bears and miniatures is that the material is rather inexpensive. In addition, you don't need much space for them.

If you want to know more about making miniatures and want to learn it step-by-step, I recommend Debbie Kessling's book, How to Make Enchanting Miniature Teddy Bears, which includes some exciting projects (such as a miniature no-no-teddy). If you are living in the United States, you can purchase her video, which shows the techniques of making minis.

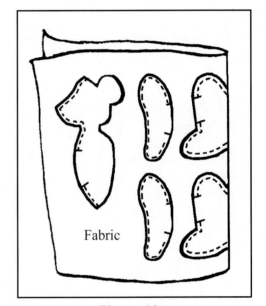

Fabric

Figure 46A.

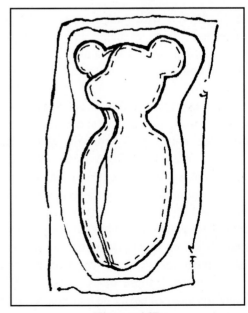

Figure 46B.

Clockwise:

21. Dollhouse bear with miniatures, 2-1/4 inches (6 cm).

22. "Berthold" is the miniature version of my "Honeybears".

23. After having made my "Honeybear" as a miniature, I tried in the beginning of 1999 to make my realistic bears as miniatures too. This was not as easy as making an ordinary mini, as the heads are very small and the tiny ears nearly drove me crazy. But my realistic miniature bears are as poseable as the large ones. I used pipe cleaners for their armatures so they could bend their legs and move their heads. Miniature American black bear, viscose, 2-1/2 inches (6 cm).

24. Miniature pandas were nominated for the TOBY Award 1999, viscose, 2 and 4 inches (5 and 10 cm). *Photograph by Christoph Buchholz.*

Materials

Different materials give bears of the same pattern totally different looks. If you work with cotton plush, the bear will look a little worn as soon as it's finished. Bears made of "sparse mohair" also look rather old, which might be interesting on special projects. Very dense mohair will look fluffier. The pile length is especially important. With short-pile material, the pattern turns out with rather dis-tinct features, like teddies made of camel hair. If you'd like to dress your bears, short-pile fabrics look better than long-pile, yet the bears look a little naked if left undressed. There is also a connection between the pile length and the size of the bear. Long-piled fabrics with a hair length of 0.8 inches (2 cms) or more are only suitable for larger bears. Small bears would look like a fur ball.

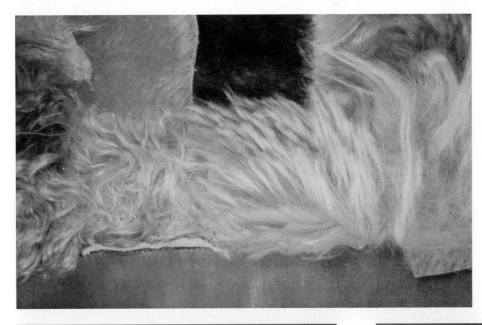

25. Mohair can come in various lengths of pile, straight or distressed, dense or sparse. *Photograph by Lars Wege.*

Below Left and Right:
26. Bears made from llama may look a little bit naked (Left), but are very good for dressing (Right).

Dyeing

Most likely you will want to make bears of different colors as well. Mohair can be purchased in a variety of colors, but you may feel tempted to dye your own fabrics. This works with special miniature bear plush and with all-natural fibers like cotton, mohair, alpaca and llama-wool, and even mohair is far less difficult than you might imagine. Viscose is good at accepting new colors too. Synthetic plush can either not be dyed at all or only with special colors.

Hand dyeing is more economical if you can purchase a length of mohair at a reduced price. Some companies offer mohair at a lower price if you buy at least one meter. You should buy light-colored mohair and then hand dye stripes of it to your heart's desire.

Dyeing takes place in a saucepan, or rather in a large electric pot, which not only holds a larger volume but also has a built-in thermostat to keep the dye at the right temperature. You can also dye in your washing machine, but this only pays off with larger amounts of fabric.

When it comes to dyeing colors, there are various natural colors, batik colors and other textile colors such as Simplicol® and Dylon® available. Like many other bear makers, I have dyed a lot of mohair in black tea because it is very easy and the colors always look very nice. Unfortunately, this method may cause deterioration in the mohair many years later because of the acid in black tea. This should be considered when determining whether you want to try tea or use another method. One of the reasons I like to dye with tea is that there is no poison in it, which may be found in other colors. Some people use food dye (like Kool-Aid®). Although it gives very bright colors and works well, its scent can attract tiny insects.

In fact, most of the time you can't be sure how some of the materials you are using will affect your teddies in years to come. I have described the problems with excelsior before. In the 1950s some large companies started to fill teddies with soft foam to make them cuddly and washable. This worked very well until it was discovered that the material alters as time goes by. It becomes clumsy and eventually turns to a kind of dirty, sticky dust. As a bear doctor, I have to replace this material with a different stuffing. I was told to wear a mask when pulling it out of the bear because it became very unhealthy. Remember - this was invented for use for babies and small children.

For the purpose of dyeing with tea, it is acceptable to use cheap blends of tea and keep the better quality for drinking. Results will vary with the choice of tea. It also depends on the amount of tea in the dye and the amount of time you allow it to soak. All the tones created with tea are usually very harmonious, so there's no risk involved of getting a bad color.

To avoid trouble with washing loose tea leaves out of my fabric, I put the tea into bags that I lock with paper clips or I use store-bought tea bags. I fill my pan with as much hot water as is necessary to move the cloth back and forth and keep it covered with water at all times. Then I add the tea and fabric. I bring the tea to the boiling point, then continue dyeing the cloth at a lower temperature. I have to stir it now and then to obtain an even color, of course (Photo 27).

After dyeing, I wash the fabric in warm water and take care that no tea is left in it, then spin-dry it and hang it out to dry. You can also use the tumble dryer. Drying outdoors influences the nap line, so you can get it to lay in the opposite direction. If you'd like to get a distressed nap, lay the mohair flat to dry after brushing in different directions. I use a nailbrush and rotate it while brushing.

It may surprise you that mohair can be boiled. Since the backing tends to shrink a little during the process, the fur gets denser and fluffier. This is why some bear makers recommend washing all new mohair furs before use. This way, you can also get rid of the stiff back dressing that English mohair often has.

Heat will not damage your mohair. However, you should avoid rubbing the fabric while washing, as it may get felted. This is especially important with alpaca.

Another natural color is turmeric (kurkuma) as it's used in the Indonesian kitchen. Turmeric produces a rich, golden yellow. It is a very strong dye, so you only need a small spoonful of the powder to dye eight inches of fabric. Turmeric may be used without adding salt or vinegar, and it dyes the backing as well as the hair.

Using red wine will result in a light grayish red. Walnuts are one of the world's oldest sources for dyeing hair in brown shades. If you cut the green fruits covering the nuts, be careful to wear gloves, or you will also dye your hands. There are, of course, lots of other natural colors. If you're interested, visit shops that offer materials to dye wool. There are also books available about dyeing with natural colors.

In trying these colors, you may find that some of them dye only the mohair but not the cotton backing. This may look quite interesting. I have tried cochineal, which results in an intense pink hair on white fabric. If you use it on yellow mohair you may get reddish brown mohair with yellow backing. The various colors of natural hair dye (like henna) will also dye only the mohair, not the backing (Photo 36).

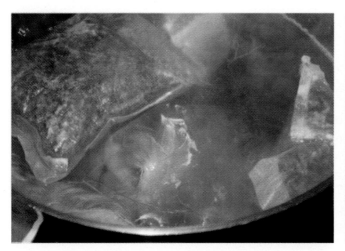

27. I had an order for a dachshund, but could not buy any fabric in the color that was required, so I had to dye it myself. Since I did not have mohair in the light gold that I needed, I dyed long-piled white mohair in black tea.

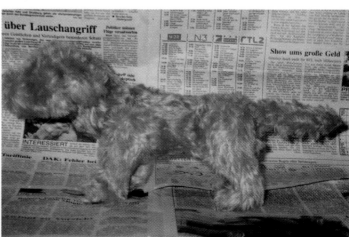

28. Next, I sewed the dachshund from the mohair I had dyed.

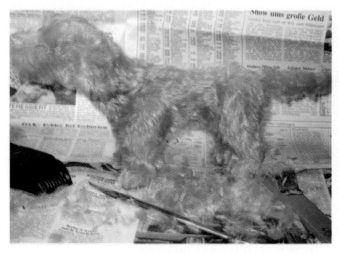

29. The dog needed some trimming before painting. Only the whiskers and brows stayed at the original length.

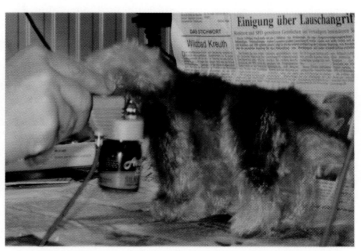

30. The dachshund was then airbrushed with a thin color made for painting on fabrics.

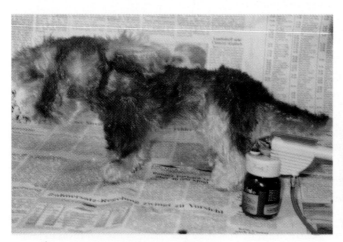

31. When the airbrushing was complete, only a few fair spots remained in the dachshund's fur.

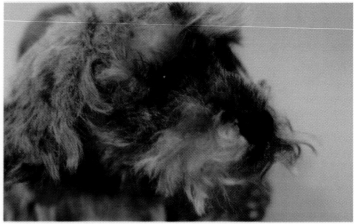

32. The color should be fixed by ironing. As this was not possible with the dog, he was dried with hot air. Now the black color turned gray.

33. An English Bulldog should have light brown areas in its fur. I sewed this one from white mohair and then painted it with silk paint.

Below:
34. To set the color, the dog was then placed in an oven-proof bag along with a wet rag. It was steamed in the oven for half an hour at 100 degrees Celsius. Coming out of the oven, the dog was a little moist, so he was dried with a hairdryer. The stuffing and joints were not harmed.

You will also find a variety of ready-to-use colors. The widest range of shades may be found in the colors made for batik clothes, which also work very well on mohair. The use of the common textile colors depends on their individual instructions. You should remember that nearly all shades of brown are more or less reddish. For example, Simplicol® brown gives a rich copper red. This is very nice, but if you'd rather have a real brown, you'll need to mix colors, either mixing the dyeing powder right before use or dyeing in stages. As you will remember from your art classes at school, you'll need to add green to the red you already have. The outcome depends on which color you use first and what shade of green you have. The second dye is always weaker than the first, as each fiber can accept color only to some degree. You can also achieve interesting results by adding gray as an extra color.

If you want to dye the cotton backing as well as the mohair, you will need to add salt for dyeing cotton and vinegar for dyeing mohair fibers. In dyeing upholstery fabric you also have to add salt.

When dyeing with store-bought colors, always follow the directions of the manufacturer. Some indicate on the package that the dye can't be used for mohair, although there is usually no problem with mohair. Since most of these colors come as a powder to mix with water, wear a mask while working with the powder. It is never good to breathe in the tiny particles.

Some colors are more lightproof than others are. It would be difficult to test them all before use. Each color,

35. The finished English Bulldog.

whether you dyed it yourself or purchased pre-dyed mohair, will bleach in sunlight. Therefore, keep your bears away from too much light, and don't display them in a sunny window.

All in all, you will have noticed that dyeing is something for bear makers keen on experimenting – I hope you're one of them.

36A

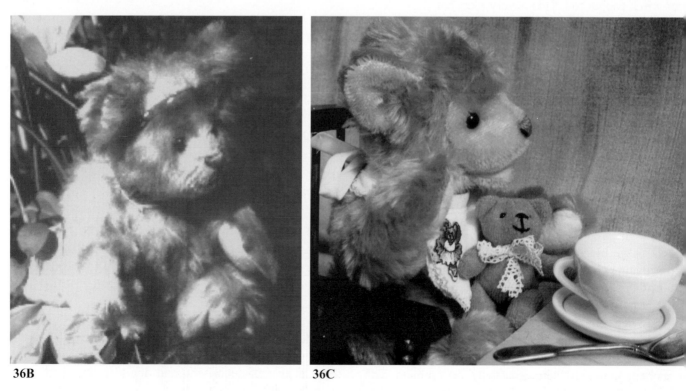

36B   36C

36. 36A. "Hannchen" was dyed with henna, which will only dye the hair, so the cotton backing remained white. 36B. "Sheila" mad
by Anna Ilisch was dyed with liquid hair color (tips only). 36C. The fur of "Joyce" was boiled in oak-boark to get the reddish brow
color. The teddies on 36D and 36E were dyed in bought fabric dye. All bears except "Sheila" were made from the same design, bu
vary in type of fur, size, and their inserted faces or open mouths.

42

36D

36E

Dyeing the Tips Only - Airbrushing

37. "Monterey" was created by Debbi Henretty. He was hand-painted using a process that she developed over a four-year period. *Photograph by Debbi Henretty.*

So-called tipped mohair is very pleasant, yet often very expensive. Tipped mohair means that the hair tips are of a different color than the lower hair. I of course had to try to create this effect myself. I did not manage to get the hair tips colored as evenly as they are with manufactured tipped mohair, but the results were very satisfying.

My first attempt was with henna, used for dyeing human hair. I laid out the strip of fabric and covered the hair tips with the henna paste. Half an hour later, I washed off the henna and ended up with a piece of mohair with reddish orange tips. For other colors, ready-bought hair tint is useful as well. I put it on a glass plate and distribute it as evenly as possible on the mohair with the aid of a small sponge rubber roller. A small sponge would also do the job (Photo 36, Sheila).

Airbrushing is another method of dyeing the tips. You can hang your fabric up and brush it, but keep an eye on the distance to get an even color. If you get too close, you will color the backing

38. Debbi Henretty's "Grizz Lee Bear" has a realistic fur that was created using batiked fabric. *Photograph by Debbi Henretty.*

as well. It's also possible to dye parts of a finished bear. If you only want to add some colored areas like eyebrows, rosy cheeks or the black eye spots of a panda, you can use a textile-marker that comes in many colors. Remember that brown tends to be reddish - you may need black as well.

The big companies create color accents with the aid of airbrush devices. Unfortunately, good airbrush equipment is very expensive. Since I don't airbrush very often, I get rather good results with an airbrush starter set. However, I have also used a simple paintbrush to color bears and animals. I have tried various colors for painting fabric and airbrushing, and have used opaque fabric paint and watered it down. Most colors specially made for airbrushing must be mixed with water or alcohol, because without it the color would be too thick and clumsy and would stick to the mohair - mohair fibers are much thinner than human hair. However, I have used liquid colors made for silk painting on mohair. You should test a small piece of your fabric first.

Some fabric colors must be fixed by ironing the back side of the fabric. If you paint a finished bear or animal this is not possible, but I've had good results using a very hot hair dryer. You can see the steps of airbrushing a finished animal on photos 27 - 32.

The colors made for painting on silk that must be fixed by steaming come out more brilliant. Sandy-Kay Murphy gave me the idea of steaming a finished animal in the oven using an ovenproof bag. This is shown on photos 33 - 35.

If you like really colorful teddies, I recommend the book, The Bear Canvas - A Guide to Fabric Painting and Teddy-Bear-Making by Australian bear makers Sandra-Kay Murphy and Bronwyn Barton. They show in 10 projects how to paint on mohair before cutting and sewing, using the steam method to set the colors.

The special charm of dyeing the fur oneself is in creating colors or color combinations that cannot be purchased in shops. It's also useful for restoring old bears if you need to get a color just like the one of an arm that's missing.

Inserted Faces

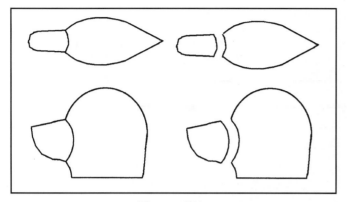

Figure 47A.

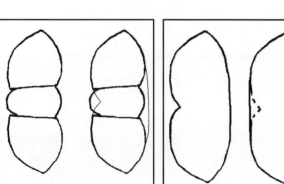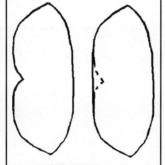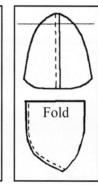

Fold

Figure 47B.   **Figure 47C.**   **Figure 47D.**

I use inserted faces more than most bear makers, as I like the special effects they will produce. An inserted muzzle of a contrasting color can change your teddy's appearance completely (Photo 39). Usually, one uses two fabrics of matching color, with the fabric for the muzzle being shorter-piled and often lighter in shade. For the muzzle, very short-piled mohair looks good, as well as llama-wool fabric. For very small bears I combine mohair and non-shiny upholstery plush, for example Munchausen (Photo 50).

The Hermann Teddy Bear Company has used the simplest form of inserted muzzles for decades. All teddy lovers know these typical Hermann bears with their bright muzzles and inner ears. The Steiff Company also works with inserted muzzles, but in a large variety of shapes. It

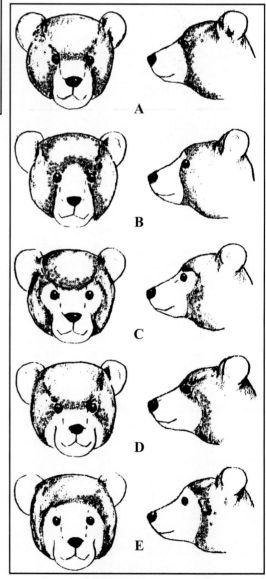

Figure 48.

pays to regard the different Steiff bears only from the aspect of the snouts' shapes.

You can use any teddy pattern to make an inserted muzzle. Simply cut a second stencil of the head parts. On these, draw the borderline, then cut the stencils according to Figure 47a. My drawing will give you an idea of the variety of possibilities (Fig. 48).

Next, the muzzle pieces are cut out of the muzzle fabric. The easiest method is used by the Hermann Company and involves sewing the muzzle pieces to the corresponding head pieces before sewing the head. Afterwards, the head is sewn as usual.

Sometimes, it looks more elegant if the muzzle is made out of a single piece of fabric. In this case, sew the rest of the head first, leaving it open at the throat-line. Now make your single muzzle stencils into one (Fig. 47b). To prevent the tip of the nose from becoming too pointed, you may round off the stencil (Fig. 47c) or sew off the tip after closing the neck seam (Fig. 47d).

Insert the muzzle piece unsewn and do not sew up the rest of the head yet. It's safer to baste in the muzzle first, and, if you chose a very curved lineage, sew it in by hand as well. Afterwards, you can close the neck seam as usual. You must, however, be careful that the muzzle and the throat meet in the same place. I usually do it like "Hermann" and make the inner ears out of the muzzle fabric as well, since I think it harmonizes. Real bears, on the other hand, often have bright muzzles, but dark ears.

39. These two mohair "Dolly" bears, 3 and 4 inches (8 and 10 cm) show the most common type of inserted muzzle (see Figure 48, type a). I usually do it without seams in the muzzle.

40. The inserted face I use very often is type "b" (Figure 48). It makes the nose a little bit longer, and the bear may look more serious like my "Mama Bear" (Left) or it may produce a funny guy like Anna's "Trolly" (Above). "Mama Bear" is 14 inches (36 cm), while "Trolly" is 8 inches (20 cm). Both are made of mohair. "Trolly". *Photograph by Lars Wege.*

47

Above Left and Right:
41. I very often need the type "b" inserted muzzle (Figure 48) for my realistic bears such as the American black bears "Batibal" and "Cinnamon"(Left). The Asiatic black bear, "Selena" (Right), shows the muzzle in a departed, but closed form. Alpaca, 8 inches (20 cm). *Photograph by Christoph Buchholz.*

42. "Aswail", portrait. Sloth bears have large, unusual lips which I designed the same way as the "English Bulldog" (Photo 35).

43. The large bear features muzzle type "d" and the small bears show the muzzle type (Figure 48).

44. "Baloo", 11-3/4 inches (30 cm), made as a one-of-a-kind for a contest, features the inserted face type "d" (Figure 48). All my versions of "Honey-bear" also feature this type of muzzle.

45. "Smokey" was one of my earliest designs. I threw away the pattern, as I did not consider it to be good. Later, I had to reconstruct him , as this bear became a success. He is 11-3/4 inches (30 cm) tall and made of mohair.

46. If I want to show persons as bears, I like to choose the type "e" inserted face (Figure 48), which produced the man-like faces on "Molly" (Top Left) and "Oliver" (Above). "J. Sanders" (Left) also features this type of muzzle. All three bears are made of mohair. "Molly" is 7 inches (18 cm) tall. *Photograph by Lars Wege.* "Oliver" is 4 inches (10 cm) tall, while "J. Sanders" is 4-1/2 inches (12 cm).

47. Both Drummers were made of the same synthetik plush. The open mouth of the right bear was inserted into a simple slit. The Drummer on the left shows an open mouth combined with an inserted face type C.

48. An open-mouth may also be combined with an inserted tongue as shown by this wolf (mohair, shoulder height 10" [25 cm]).

49. The lion is able to open or shut his mouth. To manage this, his head was designed to insert a snap used for coats. The lion and his master were designed in 1998 for the contest "Circus Bearasani" from the German magazine, "Teddybär und seine Freunde." They won second prize in the Champion's category.

Open Mouths

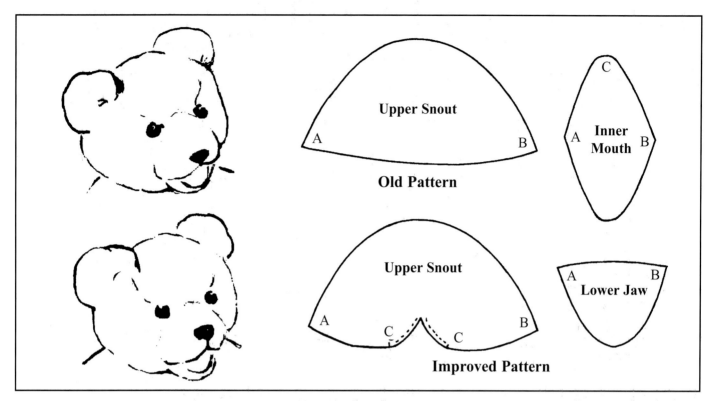

Figure 49.

The most famous open-mouthed bears are Steiff's "Zotties" and the similar bears made by other companies. These bears are usually plump with round heads, and are still very popular. However, among artist bears, open-mouthed bears are rather rare. Actually, an open mouth requires advanced abilities, yet this should not keep anyone from trying, since an occasional open-mouthed bear will bring variety into a group of bears.

Unfortunately, as far as I know, good patterns for open-mouthed bears have not yet been published. There are some patterns with the upper muzzle line flatly running downward, giving the open mouth a beak-like look, especially in profile (Photo 47). If you own a pattern like this, it's easy to change the shape of the muzzle a little (Fig. 49) so your bear will get an open mouth with an upper jaw of the right shape. In this revised muzzle piece, the snout is closed along the dotted line, then the inset is sewn onto it.

Usually, you can give any pattern an open mouth. As the picture of chatting neighbors shows, it can be quite charming to make two similar bears, one mouth open, one closed (Photo 50). The easiest way of doing so is to slit the side piece of the head and insert the felt mouth (Photo 47, Drummer right side), but you must make the slit in the right place. Just like with dogs, the mouth of a bear does not separate the upper and lower jaw right in the middle. Two thirds of the snout belong to the upper jaw and only one third to the lower jaw (Fig. 50). The inner mouth is usually made of skin-colored felt. To make it more durable, you can iron interfacing onto the back. Some fabrics, like ultrasuede or cotton velour work better for the inner mouth than felt.

Folding a piece of paper twice can create a pattern for the inner mouth. This way, you only have to draw one quarter of the inner mouth. The outer edge is just as long as the mouth slit, but of course the line is curved. You can calculate it or take the measurement with a string, or you can use a piece of wire as a rule, but I must admit that I simply draw it by eye. Once you cut the inner mouth, you'll have the pattern for the whole piece of the inset.

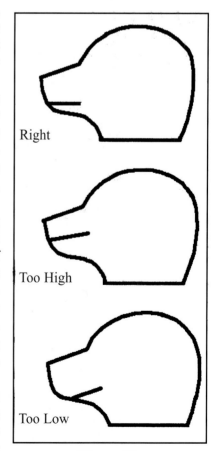

Figure 50.

50. The open mouth of "Lucky Jack" was combined with the inserted face of type "c" from Figure 47 (like the 2nd Drummers). The "Neighbears" were designed for a Dutch contest with the theme "News". Both women are made from the same pattern, except for the mouth being open or closed. They show face "B" as well as "Baron Munchausen", my third TOBY nominee. By the way, Munchausen, does not wear a wig, his pig-tail hair style is part of his head design and made of very long piled mohair.

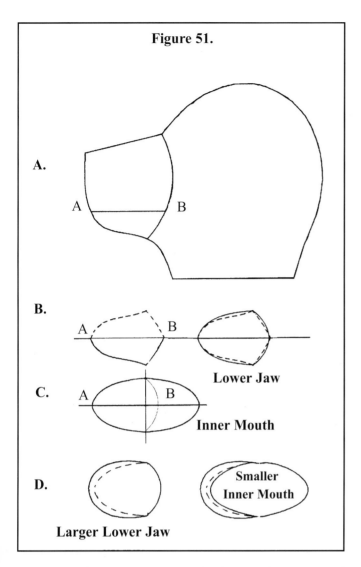

Figure 51.

A.

B.

A ⟍ B

Lower Jaw

C.

A ⟍ B

Inner Mouth

D.

Larger Lower Jaw

Smaller Inner Mouth

It is more common to combine the open mouth with an inserted muzzle. I, too, find this more elegant. Basically, all kinds of inserted muzzles can be used, but the types a, b and c on Figure 51 work best.

To get a suitable pattern, the snout's pattern is divided this time (Fig. 51a). The upper muzzle remains unchanged. However, it looks better if the lower jaw is made out of one piece. You can make a pattern by mirroring the lower jaw by the sideline, then rounding off the edges (Fig. 51b). By mirroring the lower jaw at the corner points, you'll get the pattern for the inner mouth (Fig. 51c). Mirroring is made easier by drawing half the lower jaw onto paper that has been folded twice, then simply cutting.

This method is very simple, and most bears with open mouths that you can purchase are made in this way. However, I was not quite satisfied because the division line between the inner mouth and lower jaw was always visible from the sides. My solution (Fig. 51d) is a little more complicated, but in my opinion, it looks better.

First, I take a few millimeters from the inset's size, adding them to the lower jaw. Since both parts are not of equal size any more, I have to baste the inset before I machine sew it. For very small bears, I sew the muzzle by hand.

The following steps are always the same: close the front seam of the upper jaw. Baste the upper section of the inner mouth to the upper jaw's edge, then machine or hand sew. The head pieces are already sewn together, and this time, the neck seam is closed as well. Mark the corners of the mouth when drawing out the pattern, so you'll know where to insert the muzzle. First baste, then sew in the entire muzzle. Take care to sew in the muzzle evenly and symmetrically, or the bear's mouth will look twisted (Fig. 52). The muzzle, especially the lower jaw, must be stuffed very carefully. To avoid creating a yawning mouth, sew the corners of the mouth together with a few stitches. This is also a cosmetic surgery tip for older bears with gaping jaws.

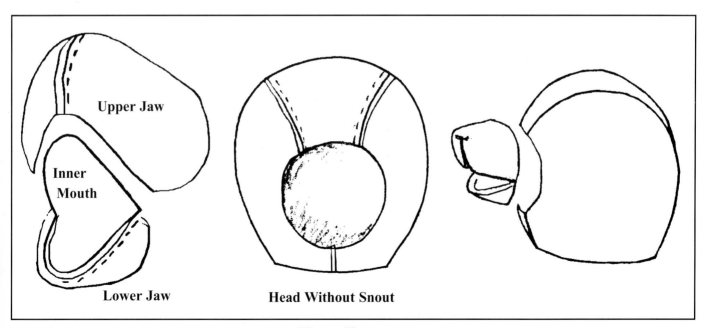

Upper Jaw

Inner Mouth

Lower Jaw

Head Without Snout

Figure 52.

Own Design

Before designing your own patterns, you should determine which types of teddies you actually prefer. Is it the classical shape of bears, resembling the old ones, or the small cuddly ones with their friendly faces? Maybe you also have a soft spot for eccentric character bears.

In bear making, you needn't specialize in one direction. For years, I have enjoyed making the most different bears between 2 and 20 inches (5 and 51 cms), among them both classical and character bears, as well as realistic four–legged bears. It's this variety that keeps me from developing too much routine and getting bored.

Anyway, it's good to compare as many bears as possible. You'll find this opportunity at teddy shows as well as in books and magazines. Regard the teddies critically. If you like one, ask yourself what it is that makes this fellow so amiable. Is it the special look or the smile? In the same way you should find out why another bear does not please you. Try to find out what was done wrong – sometimes you'll learn from other people's mistakes.

51. In September 1989 I tried my first design from scratch after having altered other patterns from the beginning. I used a very cheap synthetic because I was really unsure about the result. In fact, "Hubert" looked different from my idea, but I was really proud of him. He is 12 inches (31 cm) tall.

First Tries

In the following chapter, I'll give more detail about the development of your own patterns, but my first advice in this context might surprise you a little. Try out as many different patterns as possible. All teddy magazines frequently publish patterns you should try. The patterns are often similar, so you may learn the effect of small variations when sewing. Continuing like this, you'll finally learn to assess a teddy's looks just by regarding the pattern without needing to see the finished bear. For this state of experimentation, my daughter Maja published the Kombi pattern that you will find in this book. The various pieces of the pattern may be combined in any way, thus making any number of bears. There are two different bodies, the arm patterns, four head sides with three gussets, two different legs and three ears of various sizes. Depending on which pieces are used, a slender classical teddy may be made as well as a short–nosed chubby one.

You can easily add more pieces to this pattern. The simplest variation concerns the ears: it's no trouble to enlarge or reduce them. It's nearly just as easy to change the shape of an arm or make a belly rounder or slimmer. Things to keep in mind when altering the head's pattern are detailed in the chapter, "Head Design."

It's easier to start with small alterations like this than to draw a whole new pattern to start with. The experience you gain will help you with realizing your very own ideas later and drawing your patterns from scratch.

52. In April 1992 I used my "Hubert" pattern for "Hubertus the Hunter" (Above), a 14-inch (36 cm) bear I made out of llama for a Dutch contest. In June of the same year I got an order for "Goldilocks and the Three Bears", so I used this design for "Papa Bear", 18 inches (46 cm) and made of mohair (Right). I also made the doll, which is jointed like a teddy.

Proportions

Figure 53. Brown Bear.　　**Figure 53.** Steiff 1903.　　**Figure 53.** Cheap old bear.　　**Figure 53.** Steiff 1975.

To show you how to change an entire pattern by using your own ideas, I'd like to give three examples.

Teddies are no doubt far more gregarious than their ancestors, the wild bears, whose cannibalistic father bears are the biggest threat to the cubs. Luckily, teddies are much more peaceful and also live in real families with a father, mother and children. The idea of making a teddy family like this quickly comes to mind. Of course, children are smaller than their parents are, so it should have occurred to you that it's possible to enlarge or reduce your pattern with the help of a copy machine or scanner.

However, if you want to make a teddy family, you'll have to do more than just enlarging or reducing your pattern. With bears, just like with humans, children are not only smaller, but also have very different proportions compared to grown–ups. I will give more details in "A Teddy Child."

The first teddies had a rather large similarity to real bears: a long body with long arms, large feet and small heads. This is what is called the "classical" shape today, and it has grown quite popular again. Yet as the decades went by, teddies' proportions grew more childlike. The trunk and arms grew shorter and the head even larger and rounder (Fig. 53).

Proportions may also tell you something about a bear's origin. While the teddies of well–known companies like Steiff or Hermann were well–proportioned, the small companies tried to save material by making their bears with short, straight arms, and short feet, (Photo 60) while the heads looked bulky. Those bears may be made of mohair, but their proportions make them look like fairground bears.

53. These three teddies were made in 1990 from synthetic plush. The baby and the toddler feature the type of childlike, cuddly bears that may be nice up to 12 inches (31 cm). They are 8 and 10 inches (20 and 25 cm) tall. Their grandfather is around 19 inches (48 cm), and has a rather classic design.

54. When I made "Andi" from a pattern in a book, I was very proud. At 6 inches (15 cm) tall, this was the smallest bear I had made until then. In fact, he also has bad proportions. It was difficult to find a place to mount his arms and legs.

55. This teddy was made from a pattern I purchased, and besides a bad open mouth it has very bad proportions. The long pile of the synthetic fur makes it even worse: he looks like a big fur ball.

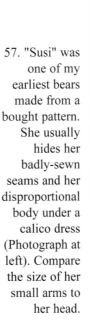

56. This group was made from bought patterns in my first year of bear making. The mother has the same design as the baby in photo 53, but she is more than 20 inches (51 cm) tall and is out of proportion.

57. "Susi" was one of my earliest bears made from a bought pattern. She usually hides her badly-sewn seams and her disproportional body under a calico dress (Photograph at left). Compare the size of her small arms to her head.

58. These two photographs show different combinations and sizes of teddies made from the Kombi pattern. The two musicians are in the original size of 10 inches (25 cm) and the teddies waving their flags are 7 inches (18 cm) tall. Kombi bears have rather classic proportions (all made by Maja Ilisch).

59. These little fellows represent the cuddly type of teddy bears. They are 8" and 10" (20 and 25 cm) and made of synthetic plush.

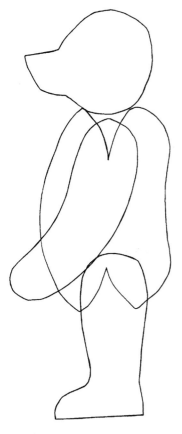
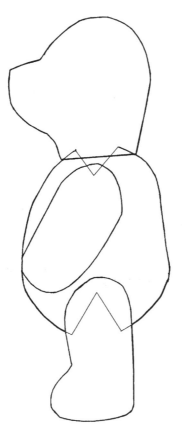
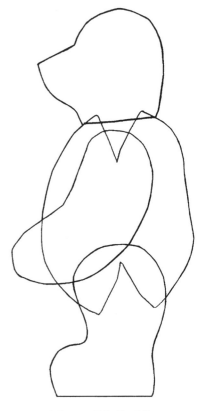

Figure 54. Classic. **Figure 54.** Bad. **Figure 54.** Cuddly.

The teddy patterns published recently in manuals and magazines differ in proportions as well. There are very nice classical patterns, such as those for cheeky cuddly bears and some interesting funny characters. Yet there are also manuals that, in my opinion, contain rather badly proportioned patterns. As a beginner, I tried out each pattern just as I found it. Once I noticed that the head did not fit the body – I had made no mistakes, but the head was simply too big. Luckily, I had enough fabric left for the head, which was actually quite nice, to get a suitable body. I gave the first body a smaller head and was the owner of two nice bears.

After this experience, I looked critically at all new patterns, learning that it is not unusual for heads to be out of proportion. If your head pattern is nearly as big as the pattern for the body, it might be that the bear has bad proportions, but you can reduce the head. Lay out your stencils like a teddy and decide which size of head you like best. If you are not certain, I would suggest that a small head always looks better than a big one. You should study the pattern for the arms carefully as well. There are very long and very short arms. The long ones can look a little apish at first, but on a finished bear they are far less unattractive than short stumps, especially when you have the option to bend them by armatures. Here is a clue for the proper arm length for an adult bear: the arm's pattern is the same length as the body or just a little shorter. On the finished bear, the arms should reach at least to the crotch. You should always design your teddy's arms slightly bent, never straight, which makes them look stiff (Fig. 54).

60. A bear with very short arms from an unknown German company.

Head Design

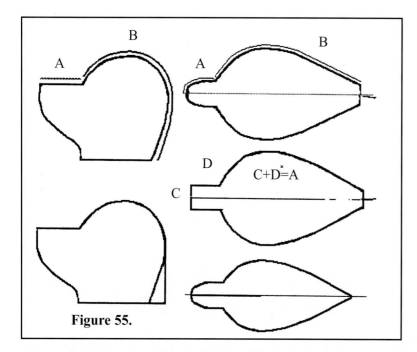

Figure 55.

The head is undoubtedly the most important part of a teddy. Sure, it must fit the shape of the body, but there are other aspects to consider as well. I've already told you how to vary the head without altering the pattern. Naturally, the head is the first part you'd like to adjust to your taste.

In most cases, mainly the muzzle is changed, growing longer or shorter. This does not create a problem with the sides of the head. You simply draw the side of the head again and then change it however you like. But what should you do about the gusset? It must, of course, be altered as well; the snout is elongated or shortened like the head side. If the head sides and gusset have a sharp dip (Fig. 55), make sure that the distance from the tip of the nose to the dip (a) equals the counterpart on the gusset. If this line bends, you can use a string or wire to take the measurements. If it has edges, simply measure out the single sections, adding up to the length of (a).

To make your new gusset symmetrical, draw only half of it onto a folded sheet of paper. By cutting, you'll arrive at the whole gusset. You may also keep the halved pattern and reverse it when drawing on the fabric. Sometimes, it's rather practical to cut the gusset in

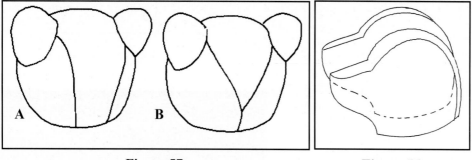

Figure 57.   **Figure 56.**

two separate parts. This type of head was used with the old bears, which are referred to as "center–seam bears." One advantage of this method was that is saved fabric when cutting out the pattern. The bears were usually very large, and the fabric could be used up more economically. In addition, this type of bear is easier to sew. Although there is an extra seam, the single seams are simpler, and therefore faster to sew. The parts of the gusset are sewn to the corresponding head sides first, which usually works without basting. Then both sides of the head are sewn together with one long seam from chin to neck (Fig. 56), (Photo 87, Christopher).

If your teddy's head needs to be wider or narrower, you can't stop with just altering the muzzle, but also must alter your gusset by making it wider or narrower. If the gusset ends abruptly at the neck (Fig. 57a), you must measure the length of the gusset and head side, making sure they match. I usually don't like measuring, thus all my gussets have a sharp end (Fig. 57b), suiting anything. But be careful! If the gusset ends rather high up, the lower part of the head becomes narrower. To avoid this, I alter the line at the far end of the head side as well (Fig. 55, bottom).

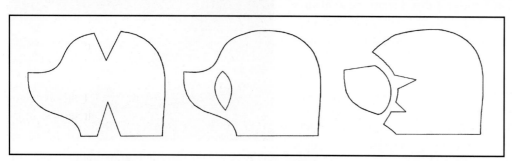

Figure 58A.   **Figure 58B.**   **Figure 58C.**

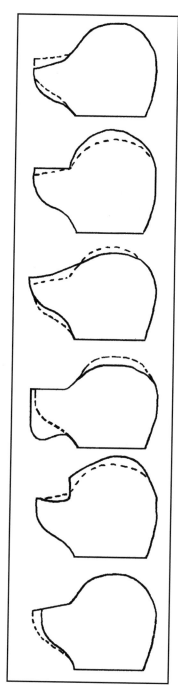

Figure 59.

Widening the gusset after the snout results in a bulkier forehead. Cheeks get rounder by adding extra darts (Fig. 58a). If you'd like to point out the change from the muzzle over to the cheeks, you may insert another dart here (Fig. 58b). You can even do this with a finished head after stuffing, but then you must be careful not to stuff too tightly. Another option for round cheeks is an inserted mouth and special darts in the head piece (Fig. 58c).

When you design a head side, don't forget that it will appear shorter than on your pattern, because a part of it will be hidden under the head. You need to add the length of your disk radius to get the size you want. If you have designed your head side too short and notice this while stuffing, there is no problem if there is a piece of your fur left. Cut a circle just slightly larger than your head disc and insert it by hand using the ladder stitch. The cotter pin will come out of the middle (Figure 11b).

These drawings are meant to show you how even small alterations of a pattern will change the look of the bear (Fig. 59). The original pattern is indicated by the dotted line. This row of head sides could go on forever, and the nose could grow longer, wider or narrower. The back of the head, which I left out in my changes, could also be designed in different ways. You may draw some more head sides, if you like. Use transparent paper and draw your own versions of the head above the basic pattern.

In Figure 60, there are three gussets that may be combined with the head sides, giving a different result each time. I restricted myself to these three simply because of space limitations. I also could have included gussets with a wider or smaller nose. You may experiment with this yourself. If you try to imagine all these heads with ears of different sizes and in different locations, you could end up with a large variety of different teddies to be made with these pieces.

As you can see, it's very simple to alter patterns this way. In the end, it's so simple that one has to ask, "What is an 'original' design?" Is it enough to take away half an inch here or add it there?

Most published patterns come with a note saying "not for commercial use." This is correct, of course, and you have to hide this, but the problem is that most classical patterns are so similar that even individual designers would hardly be able to distinguish them. Thus, if you'd enlarge the designs found in this book and use them as patterns, I would not recognize your bears as my design.

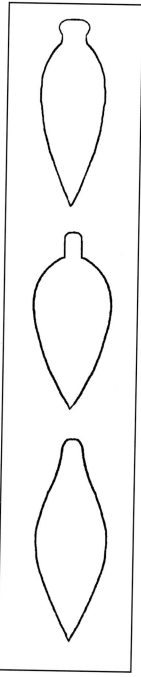

Figure 60.

I once participated in a Dutch contest in which the pattern for a mini bear was given. The results of approximately 40 contestants were exhibited afterwards, and all the teddies looked completely different.

I used lots of bought patterns to begin with and sold many of those bears since I was not aware that it was not allowed. However, in the certificates I always mentioned who had designed them, even if I had made alterations, which I usually did. *You are allowed to sell bears made from the patterns you find enclosed in this book - but tell your customers who designed them.*

Since each bear maker will have his or her own personal style, each can produce a very different teddy by using the same pattern. The problem is, some bear makers try to copy the style of other bear artists using their self-designed patterns. Try to create your own style.

In the two chapters to follow, I will tell you how to change a whole pattern by two examples. You'll find even more possibilities of designing heads apart from the classical head–side–and–gusset–method in the chapter, "Variety of Patterns". (See page 70)!

61. Dutch bear maker, 1993. *Photograph by Lars Wege.*

62. Dutch bear maker, 1993. *Photograph by Lars Wege.*

63. Teddy by "Mother Hubbard", 1992. *Photograph by Lars Wege.*

64. Teddy by "Mother Hubbard", 1992. *Photograph by Lars Wege.*

65. Annemarie van Gelderen, Netherlands, 1994.

66. Annemarie van Gelderen, Netherlands, 1994.

67. Gabriele Lepahé, Germany, 1997. *Photograph by Lars Wege.*

68. Gabriele Lepahé, Germany, 1997. *Photograph by Lars Wege.*

69. Ursula Broda, Germany, 1999.

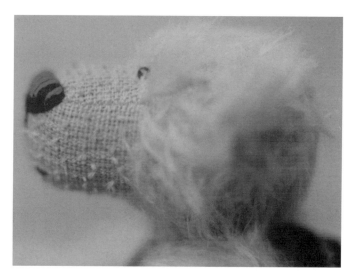

70. Ursula Broda, Germany, 1999.

71. Nelleke van den Berg, Netherlands, 1992. *Photograph by Lars Wege.*

72. Nelleke van den Berg, Netherlands, 1992.

73. Susanne Grosser, Germany, 1994. *Photograph by Lars Wege.*

74. Susanne Grosser, Germany, 1994. *Photograph by Lars Wege.*

75. Joyce Haughey, USA, 1994. *Photograph by Lars Wege.*

76. Joyce Haughey, USA, 1994. *Photograph by Lars Weg*

77. Dutch bear maker, 1992. *Photograph by Lars Wege.*

78. Dutch bear maker, 1992. *Photograph by Lars Wege.*

79. When I first wrote my book in the spring of 1996, I created the drawings concerning alterations from scratch. In the autumn of the same year, I thought it would be a good idea to try the patterns to see if they would work the way that I intended. The result was the mohair mother and her baby, 4-1/2 and 2 inches (12 and 5 cm) and the "Stan" and "Ollie" bears.

80. In March of 1999, I again used this pattern for my tableau, "Don Quixote". Using different mohair and smaller eyes with different placement resulted in the bears looking quite different. "Don Quixote", 4-3/4 inches (12 cm) is made of long-piled sparse mohair that was trimmed afterwards so he could get his thin beard. "Sancho Pansa" is also made of mohair and is 4-1/4 inches (11 cm).

A Teddy Child

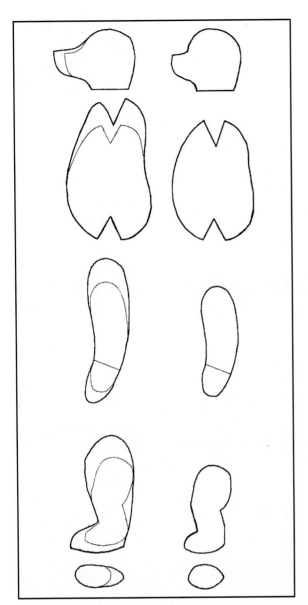

Figure 61.

Study the pattern you used, considering proportions. Do the teddies made with this pattern look childlike or grown–up?

Suppose your pattern is for a classical grown–up bear and you want to sew a baby bear. Draw out your pattern again to create a base for your new pattern. A teddy child has a shorter trunk, so you'll need to shorten the body, but don't take away the tummy. The arms may also need to be shortened a little, but not too much. They should still reach to the crotch when the cub is finished.

Draw the legs approximately the same length as the arms. If you'd like to make a teddy baby, it should have bent legs. A cub, of course, has smaller feet than a grown–up bear, so you'll need to shorten the feet and round the soles. The paws are also shorter for a teddy child (Fig. 61).

There is a rule for constructing the soles of the feet: half the circumference equals the length of the foot. You may either measure it out or estimate, like I do. Usually I draw the soles by eye below the leg pattern.

You don't have to enlarge the head – since you shrunk the body, it will already look bigger. But of course a cub has a different profile. It has a shorter snout and, compared to the grown–up, a more distinguished curved forehead.

You must also remember to shorten the gusset around the nose to match it to the new sides of the head. Transfer all the changes to your pattern, cut out the new parts and try laying them out. This will give you an idea of how the bear will look. If need be, you can make further changes now. Once you are satisfied, draw out the new pattern neatly, making it smaller if you want. The degree of reduction depends on the size the baby should have compared to the mother bear. As you can see in my drawing, it has already grown smaller because of the shorter body and legs (Fig. 62).

If you like to work with a computer and own a software program like "Photo Finish" or a similar graphic program, you can work on your scanned patterns on the computer. You can play with the pattern pieces to find out what you like. It is a lot of fun, but not necessary to create a good design.

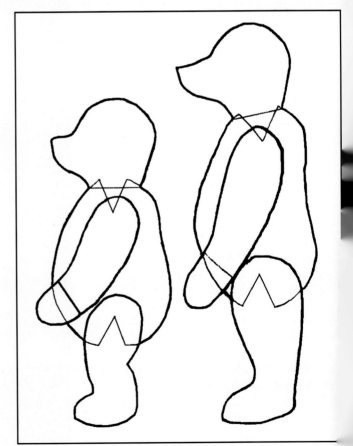

Figure 62.

Stan and Ollie

Here's another example to show you how you can alter patterns. In 1995, the magazine *Teddybär und seine Freunde* held a contest called "Teddy goes to Bearywood." It required bears portraying film figures. Imagine that you're a contestant and have decided to make Stan and Ollie. It's obvious that you can't make just any two bears in typical dress, since the success of the odd couple did in part result from the sharp contrast of their shapes.

Start up as you did before, by drawing out your "neutral" base pattern. Call to mind Stan Laurel. He was tall and slim, with a long, narrow face. Alter your pattern in this way. The tummy becomes thinner, arms and legs get longer. The head should get a profile looking more flat, maybe with a longer nose, maybe also with a narrower gusset (Fig. 63).

For Oliver Hardy, who was short and stout, the changes are quite the opposite. Don't shorten the trunk, but add a tummy. Shorten the legs, perhaps also making them fatter, but leave the feet and arms as they are since the bear should still look grown–up. The head gets a shorter nose with a profile that bends sharply. Remember to change the gusset as well. To make the head rounder, you may widen the gusset as well as create

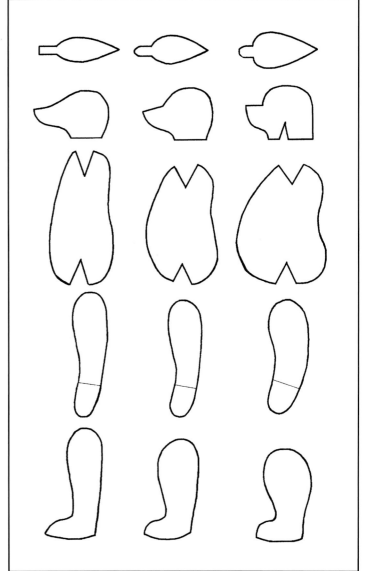

Figure 63.

chubby cheeks by adding an extra dart in the head side. Now the teddies could be taken for Stan and Ollie even if undressed (Fig. 64).

Contests like this are lots of fun. They fire the imagination and lead to teddy patterns you otherwise would never have dreamed of.

One of my most successful bears, "The Honeybear," who got a nomination, would never have been made if a friend had not told me, "Make Baloo for me."

Once you've made some bears by altering patterns, you should try drawing a pattern from scratch, then see if it turns out like you wanted. This is not too difficult when you have gained some experience in bear making. Then you will design your very own patterns.

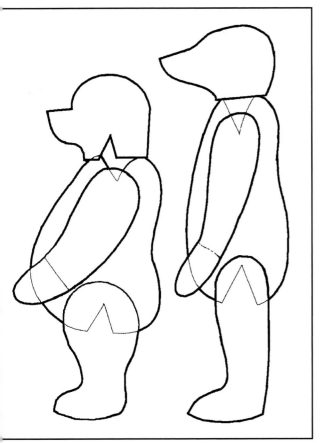

Figure 64.

Variety of Patterns

Up until now, all of my annotations referred to the "classical" base pattern: two or four body parts, outer arms, inner arms and paws, legs with soles, two head sides with a gusset going to the tip of the nose, and ears. I used this scheme since I thought it most likely that you would use patterns like this.

There are various possibilities to design teddies' heads and bodies, of course. It pays to view Steiff bears and study their design. You'll find a great variety with very interesting solutions.

Figure 65.

Let's start with the head. There is no rule stating that it must consist of the common side parts and center gusset. The most important factor is the proper shape of the head. For example, if you want to make the head in two parts without darts showing on the profile, the back of the head will be too flat. If you have ever sewn tight–fitting clothing you already know that you create the shape of the body with darts. This means that it is possible to sew a two–part head

Figure 66.

if you give it enough volume with the aid of darts. I like working with patterns like that (Photos 81, and 83). The darts are sewn up first, then the entire head can be finished with one long seam. compared to the sometimes painstaking insertion of a gusset this is quick work (Fig. 65). The larger dollhouse bear pattern in this book is like this.

I used another kind of head design in my classes with good results. In this one, there are no darts, but the back of the head gets volume through an ellipse–shaped gusset that does not go down to the nose, but begins at the end of the muzzle (Photo 82 and the groom on photo 26). also gives advantages in sewing, too. The gusset is sewn to one side of the head first, then the head is once again finished with one long seam. The Eduard Cramer Company used this kind of head pattern for a long time, giving them a typical design. I found the idea in the highly recommendable book <u>Classic Teddy Bear Design</u> by Estelle A. Worrell (Fig. 66).

Estelle A. Worrell also shows that the common three parts can be distributed in a different way: two parts, facing each other for the front profile, and one part for the back of the head (Photo 84, Anna's bears). Again, darts may be used to prevent it from looking too flat (Fig. 67a). I prefer patterns like this for my simple small "dollhouse bears," they offer the opportunity to integrate ears into the head pattern and separate them with one seam (Fig. 67b). You will find a pattern like this in my book.

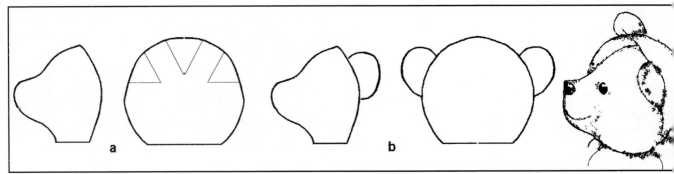

Figure 67A.

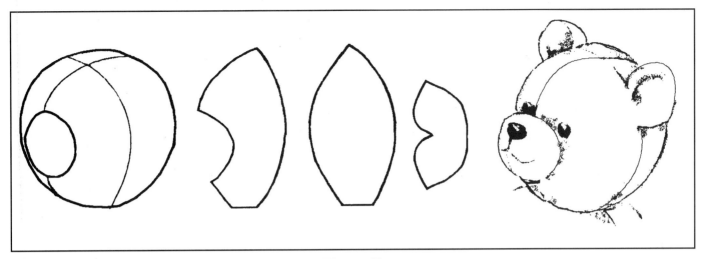

Figure 68.

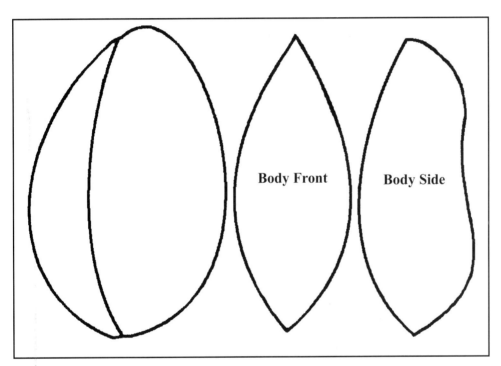

Body Front   Body Side

Figure 69.

Arm

Arm

Figure 70.

If you imagine a round teddy head, you can of course divide it into four equal parts. The two front parts have a crescent–shaped opening to insert the muzzle (Fig. 68), (Photo 85).

These are only some of the possibilities of head design. Naturally, there are countless variations. Adding inserted faces and open mouths gives you a large realm for experimentation. Perhaps you have noticed that I constantly try to experiment with any new idea. Honestly, so many bears made with the same scheme sometimes bore me.

The body need not consist of just two or four parts either. Again it's the Steiff Company that shows, especially with their cuddly bears, that three parts make sense as well (Fig. 69), such as with the children's teddy "Petsy." His pal "Zotty" had a horizontal separation in the tummy gusset, so it looked as though he were wearing a bright napkin.

"Zotties" also did not have the common shape of arms consisting of an outer arm, inner arm and paw. They had two identical arm pieces, with the paw inserted from below (Fig. 70). I prefer this type of arm pattern for my realistic bears. They are not meant to stand on the sides of their hands, but on four paws. "The Honeybear" has paws pointing down like this, too, but since he can move his arms with wire inlays, he can maintain a less cramped posture, unlike the "Zotty" bears (Photo 86).

81. In April 1991 I tried another pattern from scratch. I wanted to make a teddy head with only two pieces. I knew, of course, that I had to add darts to make the head round enough. This time I was bold enough to make my prototype from mohair. This 10-inch (25 cm) "Hannchen" became my standard pattern for child-type bears. You will find her in the section about variations or in the 5-1/2 inch (14 cm) baby version with her brother "Linus".

82. Miniature bear with ellipse-shaped gusset. I have used the heads with this type of gusset in many variations and sizes. They work very well in small bears since the gusset is easier to sew.

83. "Mama Bear", "Linus" 9-3/4 inches (25 cm), and "Baby Hannchen", 6 inches (15 cm). In fact, the pattern for "Linus" came from "Hannchen". His head was designed like hers, with an inserted face type "c" (Figure 48), combined with an open mouth. Like "Baby Hannchen", he has bent legs. Unique to "Linus" are his thumbs that he can suckle. "Lucky Jack" and the drummer are big brothers of "Linus" regarding their patterns. Heads with two pieces have been my favorite patterns for years. I like to use them for the dollhouse bears as well as for realistic bears or other animals such as the rat or the mole.

84. In the winter of 1994, my daughter Anna tried her own first design at 14 years old. She created small bears with two front head pieces and one back head piece. "Snow White and the Seven Dwarfs" (Above) were made following this design as well as "Thornrose and her Prince" (Below), of mohair. One year later, Anna used the "Snow White" design to make "Magenta" (Right) of mohair, 6 inches (15 cm). They don't wear wigs; the backs of their heads are made from long-piled black plush.

85. "Kari", the toddler on the left, has a head made of four pieces with an inserted mouth as shown in Figure 68. The teddy in the middle has a head that is not described in the text. It consists of one rather flat back piece combined with three pieces for the front and an inserted snout. I did not design this pattern and I only used it for this bear.

86. My original "Honeybear" is 12 inches (31 cm) tall. I have downsized the pattern so the tiniest version, 2-1/2 inches (6 cm), can sit on his paw. My "Honeybears" feature a three-piece-body and arms (shown on Figure 69 and 70).

87. "Christopher" is a very classical teddy featuring a center seam in his gusset. He is 15-1/2 inches (39 cm) tall and is made from a feathery, curly mohair.

Bears and Other Animals

All the instructions I have given until now were mostly meant for teddies. In 1992, I had the idea to design a bear that would look like a real one. He should also be able to imitate the many positions of real bears. I had never seen a bear like this and I did not know if it would be possible, but I tried again and again and learned through my mistakes. It took me more than three years, but at last I succeeded with "Nanook," my first realistic bear that I was content with. "Nanook" became one of my most successful bears and got a TOBY nomination in 1995.

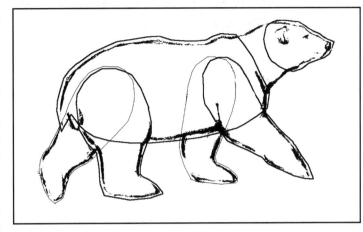

Figure 71.

For some years, I did not know who else was working on this type of design. When my polar bear was ready, I noticed that some other bear makers had also worked on designs for realistic bears; for example, Gregory Gyllenship, Dimph van Gemert and Denis Shaw, who also showed their realistic bears in 1995. Now many bear makers want to create realistic bears. If you would like to try it, too, please remember that this is one of the most difficult things to do in bear making and you need some experience. Nevertheless, try it -- it's a challenge! Do it the Richard Steiff way and observe the living models as closely as possible. Today we have the advantage of being able to watch bears not only in the zoo, but also through photographs and videos.

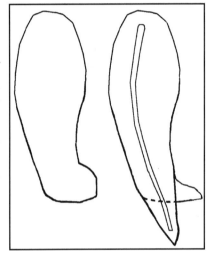

Figure 72. In designing realistic bears, the front legs are often designed like the legs of a teddy bear (see also the photograph of my first try). The result is a rather plump leg. In fact, a bear walks on his flat hand. If his front leg (arm) is designed stretched out and gets armatures, the bear may use his arms like a real one, especially being able to bend his hands in different directions.

Even with the old, classical teddies based on the brown bear, there are strong differences. The head of a grown–up bear is, to a bear maker, surprisingly small. The bear has a thick neck, a long trunk and a short tail. I already mentioned the bear's face with its big nose and narrow eyes.

You should also think about which kind of bear you'd like to make. A polar bear is by no means a white brown bear. It is so used to living in water that the shape of its body has changed a little. A panda is not simply a black–and–white speckled bear and each kind has its own proportions.

To design the pattern for a naturalistic bear, it is best if you don't use a common teddy pattern as a base. Get photos picturing the whole bear in profile, then draw the outline on transparent paper. Try to determine the shape of the thighs as well (Fig. 71).

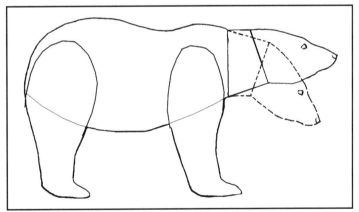

Figure 73. Using a double-jointed neck where the joint disks are not parallel, turning the whole neck-piece will allow the bear to raise or bow the head while turning the entire neck.

Now you've got the base for your bear's pattern, and the proportions should be correct. For the final pattern you must remember that a bear is not flat, and you'll need to add a little to the body and the legs for volume. You should design a suitable head gusset or work with darts. The right soles won't be any trouble, I hope. The arms must be designed like those shown in the picture. I usually design the paws stretched out, so my bears can bend them as needed (Fig. 72).

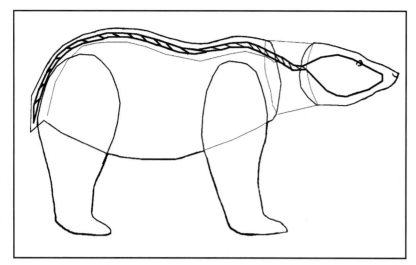

Figure 74. A "spine" allows the bear to move his head like a real bear. If you insert the "spine" into the seam allowance, as Shelly Haugen suggests, the bear will also be able to bend the back slightly if it is not stuffed too tightly. The neck piece is sewn on by hand after stuffing the body. It may be stuffed only slightly.

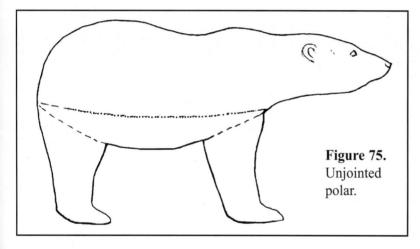

Figure 75. Unjointed polar.

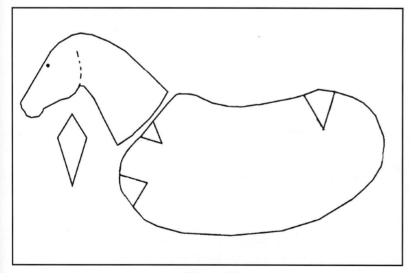

Figure 76.

You'll need an extra piece for the neck, which can be mounted with disks or molded to the head and the body to get a double-jointed neck (Fig.73). You can also insert a wire as a "spine" running from nose to tail (Fig. 74). In this case, you sew on the neckpiece by hand. To make this neck movable it may only be stuffed rather loosely, whereas the double-jointed neck must be stuffed firmly.

If you don't want your bear to be movable, draw the side of the body with the legs attached to it. You'll then need a pattern for the underbelly with the inner legs attached to it (Fig. 75). You can orient yourself with the stuffed animals you own.

As a bear maker, you'll frequently give teddies away as gifts, causing lots of joy. But what if you have friends who are less interested in bears than, say in hippos, elephants, or pigs? In cases like this, it's better to make a one–of–a–kind animal of the desired type. It's also a good idea to give a teddy an animal companion, perhaps as a special project. To make patterns, proceed just as I described for real bears. First, determine the individual qualities of the animal and try to get a suitable picture -- you may need to bring it to the right size first.

It's nearly as difficult to make an unjointed animal as a jointed one. You will need more fabric for unjointed animals, since you can't lay it as economically. Many animals, like horses or cats, have rather thin legs. It works better if you insert armatures so they won't bend under the body's weight.

The main problem is the question of how to bring a two-dimensional picture into a plastic animal. But if you're accustomed to the various ways of designing, you do not have to think about where to put the darts for long, and the work will be as easy as if you had always been working with the same pattern.

When designing other animals, you should be familiar with the use of darts and gussets to "sculpture" the head and body. For example, if you want to make a horse, you will know there will be no head-joint. Since the neck is thin compared to the body, you must form the body by darts before you can sew on the neckpiece (Fig. 76).

The shape of the head gusset will be quite different and the eyes will be set at the widest point. Perhaps you will "needle sculpture" the stuffed head and neck at the marked line.

You will find that one picture will not be enough to design an animal because you should know what it looks like from all sides. Before you start to design an animal, try to learn as much as possible about the species.

Your first own design is a very exciting thing, but nevertheless all new designs are exciting. My first "own" teddy actually looked a little different than I imagined. But I was very proud of it and I still use the pattern today. Being afraid of mistakes, I used a cheap synthetic fur, doing poor "Hubert" little good (Photo 51). Now I also make my prototypes out of good material. If you're afraid of wasting good mohair in your experiments, you may decide to use llama wool for the prototypes. If you're lucky, you'll find an old coat to recycle. A short–piled material like this shows the advantages and disadvantages of a design clearly, since nothing is hidden beneath masses of hair.

If you decide to use mohair, simply make the bear a little smaller so you'll need less of the high–quality fabric.

Each teddy you design will probably not be as you intended. But don't be afraid of accidents! Years ago I wanted to make a bear with a rather long nose and an open mouth. I did not like the finished head at all – the snout looked like a beak! Without further thought, I took out the inner mouth and stitched the muzzle up. The teddy was given a hanky and a ranger's hat and was called "Smokey." (Photo 45). Still rather doubtful, I took him to my first big bear show in Amerongen, Netherlands. Of all my bears, it was "Smokey," my outsider, who was the great winner. A well–known collector bought him and a shop ordered a number of specimens. Upon my return home, I had to reconstruct the pattern, since I had thrown it away in the meantime.

So don't throw away your first patterns. Don't forget to mark each piece, not only with the teddy's name but also with the size. A hanging file is a good place to store the patterns. I place each design of varying sizes in one folder. Every variation of that design is kept in its own clear plastic bag in this case. Patterns for miniatures are well stored in small plastic albums used for photographs, as Heike Boam suggests.

Now it's your turn, or your pattern. Don't forget: practice makes perfect when it comes to bears. You can work slowly towards your own designs, as I explained in this manual. But be daring! Be experimental! Try out new ideas! Even if you don't succeed at the first attempt, the end result will be a bear of your own. Good luck!

88. In the spring of 1992, I decided to design a bear that looked like a real one. I was not content with my first attempt. The bear was acceptable while sitting (Above), but when standing he was only a teddy on all fours (Left).

89. In the autumn of 1994, many try-outs later, I made a mother with cubs (Left). They look more like real bears, and the legs are poseable by armatures. However, the profile shows that the bear's head is too large (Below). My experiment to integrate the neck into the pattern for the head and to get more movement by using a swivel head did not work well.

90. This bear was made from the same mohair as the mother with her cubs. The smaller head and the neck make her look more realistic.

91. In January 1995, I first tried to make a polar design with the help of photographs. I was surprised to see that the head was so small, but the bear came out as I intended. The "spine" and the poseable legs allow nearly every position of real bears.

Right:
92. Asiatic black bear.

93. American black bears.

94. Even "PiXiu", a panda hugging her baby, is able to lie down or stand on four legs.

95. "Junior", a brown bear cub, is like all my bears made very poseable by using armatures.

96. "Free bears" 16" and 8" (40 and 20 cm) were made of alpaca for the Libearty-Auction at Christie's in December 1997.

97. "Aswail" and "Jungle Joker". Sloth Bears use to carry their babies on their back.

98. If you'd like to design animals other than bears, glove puppets are very easy to start with. Since the body will always be the same, you can concentrate on the head design. Dogs are the easiest animals to design. Their heads have the shape of teddy heads if you don't include the ears. My daughter Anna made both of these dogs using different parts of the Kombi pattern and designing new ears.

99. This reindeer was fully designed by Anna Ilisch. Its head shows the classic design with head sides and gusset.

All photos on this page and top photos on page 84.
100. These animals are all jointed like teddy bears. I have made many animals since I like the challenge in each new design. There are unlimited possibilities, and you can even create animals not existent in reality.

101.*Top to bottom:* The wolves are made of airbrushed mohair, their shoulder height is 10" (25 cm). The four musicians of Bremen were made of alpaca and mohair. The shoulder height of the donkey is 8" (20 cm). Toad, Ratty and Mole from "The Wind in the Willows" on their boat trip. The aminals have a size of 3" and 4" (8 cm and 10 cm). I was lucky to find a boat which fits them.

Dollhouse Bear

Above:
102. Mini bears 1-1/2-inch to 3 inches (4 to 8 cm).

Above:
103. Dollhouse bears as bride and groom, both 6 inches (15 cm), slightly larger than the included pattern.

104. Cotton dollhouse bears, 2-1/2 inches (6 cm).

Patterns For Dollhouse Bears

Minibear Pattern

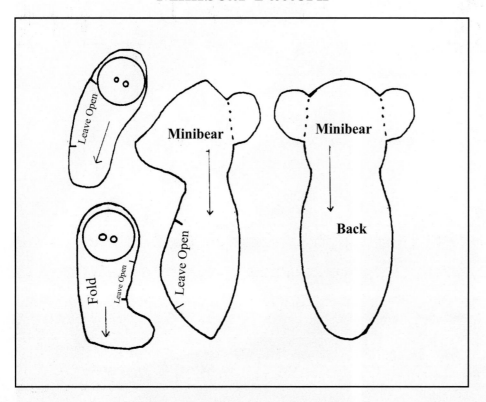

You will find information about these dollhouse bears on page 36. They are quick and easy to sew, and can be made from different materials. To get real teddies from these patterns, you can separate the head and add paws and soles. You can also enlarge and resize the patterns to get a teddy family.

Please note:
Patterns do not include seam allowance.

Dollhouse Bear Pattern

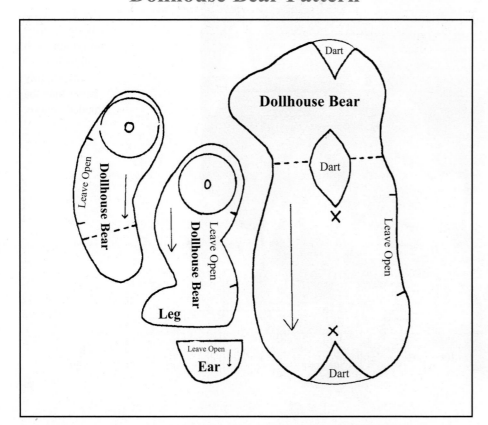

Above Left:
105. These 5-1/2 inch (14 cm) dollhouse bears were both made from the same pattern. The left bear is made from viscose, while the brown one at right is made of short-piled mohair and is fully jointed with paws and soles.

Above Right:
106. Dollhouse Bears, 2-1/2 inches (6 cm) and "Lamahaas", 3 inches (8 cm) are made of wool.

107. Dollhouse Bear "Robin Hood" is 5-1/2 inches (14 cm) and made of viscose. His horse is made of mohair.

108. Three-inch (8 cm) viscose, made from the Minibear pattern.

109. These bears range from 2 to 7 inches (5 to 18 cm) and are made of velour and cotton. All were made from the Minibear pattern.

110. Llama dollhouse bears, 3 and 4 inches (8 and 10 cm). All were made from the Minibear pattern.

Kombi Bear

111. We have created bears from the Kombi pattern in various sizes and different materials. The pattern features a rather classic-style teddy, especially "Börries", the largest of the Kombis at 16 inches (41 cm). He is made of llama.

112. "Ophelia" (Below Left) and "Archaeologist" (Below Right), both 10 inches (25 cm) were created of mohair by Maja Ilisch using the Kombi pattern. Both are traditional teddies, using head sides 2 and 3 combined with gusset 2 and 3.

Kombi Bear Pattern

by
Maja Ilisch

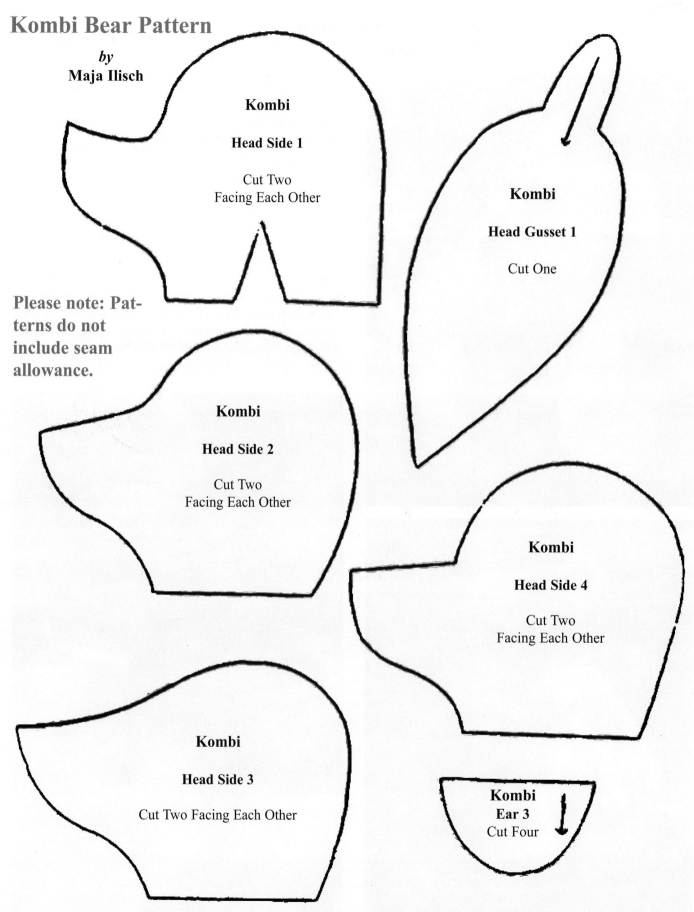

Please note: Patterns do not include seam allowance.

Kombi

Head Side 1

Cut Two
Facing Each Other

Kombi

Head Gusset 1

Cut One

Kombi

Head Side 2

Cut Two
Facing Each Other

Kombi

Head Side 4

Cut Two
Facing Each Other

Kombi

Head Side 3

Cut Two Facing Each Other

**Kombi
Ear 3**
Cut Four

You are allowed to resize the pattern or to alter the pieces as you like. If you want to sell bears from this pattern, even if you have altered them, tell your customer who the original designer was.

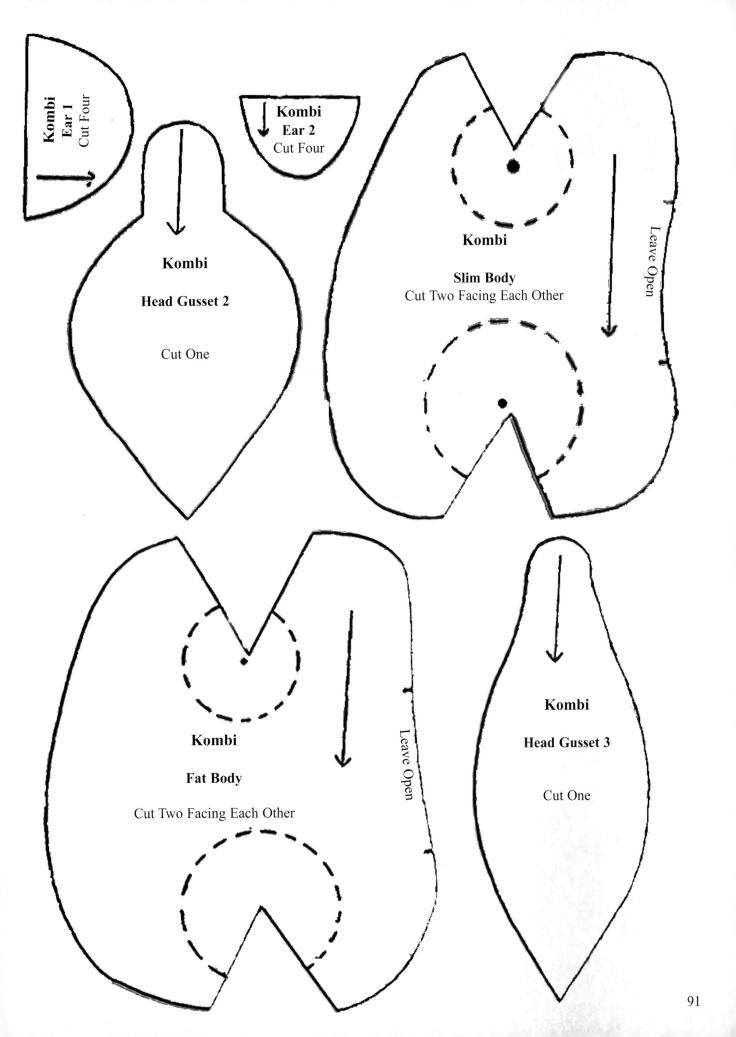

Kombi
Ear 1
Cut Four

Kombi
Ear 2
Cut Four

Kombi

Head Gusset 2

Cut One

Kombi

Slim Body
Cut Two Facing Each Other

Leave Open

Kombi

Fat Body

Cut Two Facing Each Other

Leave Open

Kombi

Head Gusset 3

Cut One

91

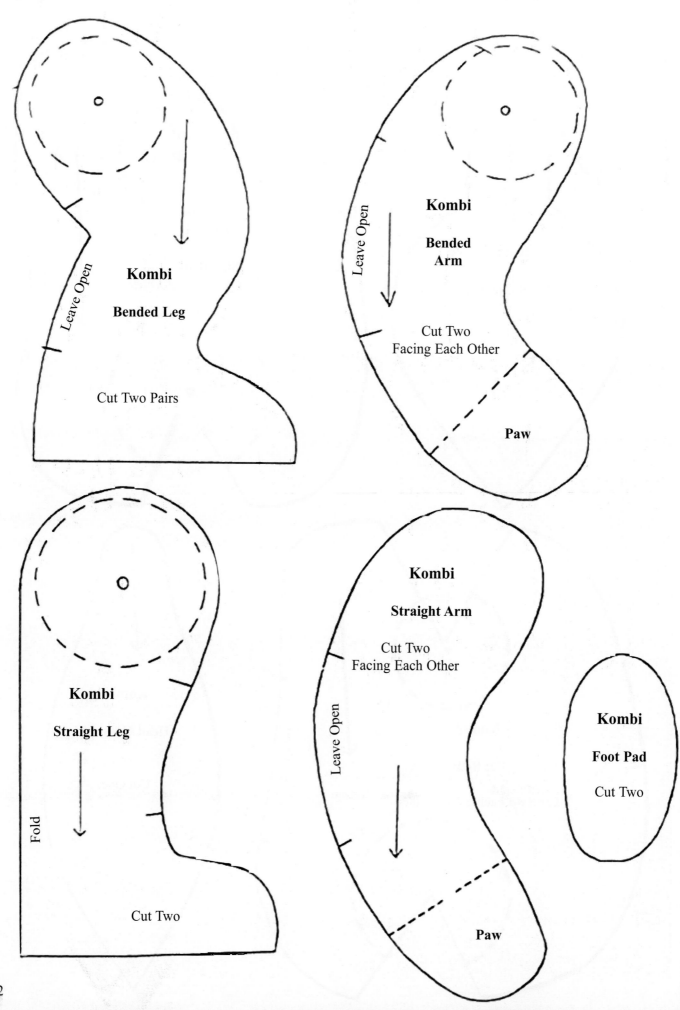

Kombi

Bended Leg

Cut Two Pairs

Leave Open

Kombi

Bended Arm

Cut Two
Facing Each Other

Leave Open

Paw

Kombi

Straight Leg

Cut Two

Fold

Kombi

Straight Arm

Cut Two
Facing Each Other

Leave Open

Paw

Kombi

Foot Pad

Cut Two

113. Three more mohair bears that Maja Ilisch created from the Kombi pattern are "Oliver" (Left) "Helios" (Below Left), both 12 inches (31 cm). They show the short-nosed variation (head side 4 combined with gusset 2).

Below:
114. "Rumpelshlzchen" is 7 inches (18 cm) and made of mohair. (Maja Ilisch).

115. Two of my bears that follow the Kombi pattern include a bear in the bathtub (Above Left) and a musician with a bass (Above Right). Both use head side 1 combined with gussets 1 and 2. They are 9 inches (23 cm) and made of mohair.

116. Anna Ilisch's Kombi mohair dwarfs are 6 and 4-1/2 inches (15 and 12 cm).

Top Left:
117. Mini Kombi pattern bear by Rotraud Ilisch, 3 inches (8 cm), mohair.

Top Right:
118. Anna Ilisch's miniature Kombi bear is 2 inches (5 cm) tall and made of upholstery plush. *Photograph by Lars Wege.*

119. A 2-inch (5 cm) Kombi miniature made by Anna Ilisch of upholstery plush. *Photograph by Lars Wege.*

About the Author

Rotraud Ilisch retired as a teacher of mentally handicapped children after she had four children of her own. She always loved drawing and crafts, and started a business making and selling cloth dolls when her children were small.

In 1987 she made her first teddy bear and soon became a professional bear maker. She taught bear making classes, sold her bears at craft shows, and created her own designs. When the German teddy bear scene was established, she became affiliated with other well-known makers. She was eager to try new things, and as the years went by her own personal style of bear making was developed. She makes classic bears, character bears, miniatures, realistic bears, and all kinds of other animals and has received prizes and TOBY nominations.

A natural extension of her teaching is writing about bears. In 1995 she published a booklet about making small bears and miniatures. Then she began A Bear of My Own for "advanced bear makers who want to learn more than the things shown in books for beginners." She says "I wrote the book I would have liked to read after having made my first bears." The book grew with the feedback she received: drawings were added, changes made, and it was translated into English.

"I am in touch with bear makers all over the world now and have learned that those who take bear making seriously always take any opportunity to learn more about the subject. I have no fear they will moan about 'just another bear making book,' Ilisch explains."

Bibliography

Estelle A. Worrell
Classic Teddy Bear Design - Heirlooms to Make and Dress
Hobby House Press, Cumberland 1988

Debbie Kessling
How to Make Enchanting Miniature Teddy Bears
North Light Books, Cincinnati, Ohio 1997

Sandra-Kay Murphy / Bronwyn Barton
The Bear Canvas - A Guide to Fabric Painting and Teddy-Bear Making
Hyde Park Press, Adelaide, South Australia 1998